Richard A. Epstein, Jr., MA
D. Patrick Zimmerman, PsyD
Editors

On Transitions from Group Care: Homeward Bound

On Transitions from Group Care: Homeward Bound has been co-published simultaneously as *Residential Treatment for Children & Youth*, Volume 20, Number 2 2002.

Pre-publication REVIEWS, COMMENTARIES, EVALUATIONS . . .

"**O**UTSTANDING, EXTREMELY USEFUL. . . . Identifies the most efficacious medication regimes for various disorders. . . . Helps youth develop skills needed to live in their community. . . . Demonstrates how to involve families in treatment. . . . Describes how an agency can partner with families and significant others in the community to help them become the supportive environments youngsters need to successfully re-enter their communities. . . . Zimmerman's masterful review of social and living skills training programs is A MUST-READ FOR ANYBODY WORKING WITH TROUBLED YOUTH."

Robert B. Bloom, PhD
Executive Director
Jewish Children's Bureau of Chicago

The Haworth Press, Inc.

On Transitions
from Group Care:
Homeward Bound

On Transitions from Group Care: Homeward Bound has been co-published simultaneously as *Residential Treatment for Children & Youth*, Volume 20, Number 2 2002.

The *Residential Treatment for Children & Youth* Monographic "Separates"

Below is a list of " separates," which in serials librarianship means a special issue simultaneously published as a special journal issue or double-issue *and* as a "separate" hardbound monograph. (This is a format which we also call a "DocuSerial.")

"Separates" are published because specialized libraries or professionals may wish to purchase a specific thematic issue by itself in a format which can be separately cataloged and shelved, as opposed to purchasing the journal on an on-going basis. Faculty members may also more easily consider a "separate" for classroom adoption.

"Separates" are carefully classified separately with the major book jobbers so that the journal tie-in can be noted on new book order slips to avoid duplicate purchasing.

You may wish to visit Haworth's Website at . . .

http://www.HaworthPress.com

. . . to search our online catalog for complete tables of contents of these separates and related publications.

You may also call 1-800-HAWORTH (outside US/Canada: 607-722-5857), or Fax 1-800-895-0582 (outside US/Canada: 607-771-0012), or e-mail at:

getinfo@haworthpressinc.com

On Transitions from Group Care: Homeward Bound, edited by Richard A. Epstein, Jr., MA, and D. Patrick Zimmerman, PsyD (Vol. 20, No. 2, 2002). *Examines ways to help prepare young people for a successful transition from group care to community living.*

Innovative Mental Health Interventions for Children: Programs That Work, edited by Steven I. Pfeiffer, PhD, and Linda A. Reddy, PhD (Vol. 18, No. 3, 2001). *"AN EXTREMELY VALUABLE RESOURCE FOR PSYCHOLOGISTS AND OTHER MENTAL HEALTH PROFESSIONALS. Clear and concise . . . strong emphasis on validation. I would recommend this book to anyone wishing to expand his/her role in treating children or anyone who now treats those with typical childhood problems but would like to do better." (David L. Wodrich, PhD, ABPP, Department of Psychology, Phoenix Children's Hospital; Clinical Associate Professor of Pediatrics, The University of Arizona Health Sciences Center)*

The Forsaken Child: Essays on Group Care and Individual Therapy, by D. Patrick Zimmerman, PsyD (Vol. 18, No. 2, 2000). *"A MUST READ for anyone concerned about the quality of care of disturbed children and youth. Zimmerman is truly the 'great chronicler' and the 'keeper of the flame' of quality group care." (Robert B. Bloom, PhD, Executive Director, Jewish Children's Bureau, Chicago, Illinois)*

Family-Centered Services in Residential Treatment: New Approaches for Group Care, edited by John Y. Powell, PhD (Vol. 17, No. 3, 2000). *Offers suggestions and methods for incorporating parents and youths into successful treatment programs in temporary and long-term settings. This essential guide will help psychologists, therapists, and social workers unite theory and practice to create a family-oriented environment for troubled clients and provide effective services. Containing case studies, personal discoveries, and insights about the potentials and limitations of residential care, this reliable resource will help you develop improved services for youths with the help of their families using reevaluated techniques to meet individual needs.*

The New Board: Changing Issues, Roles and Relationships, edited by Nadia Ehrlich Finkelstein, MS, ACSW, and Raymond Schimmer, MAT (Vol. 16, No. 4, 1999). *This innovative book offers very specific, real life examples and informed recommendations for board management of nonprofit residential service agencies and explains why and how to consider redesigning your board form and practice. You will explore variations of board structures, managed care pressure, increased complexity of service, reduced board member availability, and relevant theoretical discussions complete with pertinent reports on the practice of boards in the nonprofit residential service field.*

Outcome Assessment in Residential Treatment, edited by Steven I. Pfeiffer, PhD (Vol. 13, No. 4, 1996). *"Presents a logical and systematic response, based on research, to the detractors of residential treatment centers." (Canada's Children [Child Welfare League of Canada])*

Residential Education as an Option for At-Risk Youth, edited by Jerome Beker, EdD, and Douglas Magnuson, MA (Vol. 13, No. 3, 1996). *"As a remarkable leap forward, as an approach to child welfare, it is required reading for professionals–from child care workers to administrators and planners–or for anyone in search of hope for children trapped in the bitter problems of a blighted and disordered existence. . . . It is instructive, practical, and humanistic." (Howard Goldstein, DSW, Professor Emeritus, Case Western Reserve University; Author,* The Home on Gorham Street)

When Love Is Not Enough: The Management of Covert Dynamics in Organizations that Treat Children and Adolescents, edited by Donna Piazza, PhD (Vol. 13, No. 1, 1996). *"Addresses the difficult question of 'unconscious dynamics' within institutions which care for children and adolescents. The subject matter makes for fascinating reading, and anyone who has had experience of residential institutions for disturbed children will find themselves nodding in agreement throughout the book." (Emotional and Behavioural Difficulties)*

Applied Research in Residential Treatment, edited by Gordon Northrup, MD (Vol. 12, No. 1, 1995). *"The authors suggest appropriate topics for research projects, give practical suggestions on design, and provide example research reports." (Reference & Research Book News)*

Managing the Residential Treatment Center in Troubled Times, edited by Gordon Northrup, MD (Vol. 11, No. 4, 1994). *"A challenging manual for a challenging decade. . . . Takes the eminently sensible position that our failures are as worthy of analysis as our successes. This approach is both sobering and instructive." (Nancy Woodruff Ment, MSW, BCD, Associate Executive Director, Julia Dyckman Andrus Memorial, Yonkers, New York)*

The Management of Sexuality in Residential Treatment, edited by Gordon Northrup, MD (Vol. 11, No. 2, 1994). *"Must reading for residential treatment center administrators and all treatment personnel." (Irving N. Berlin, MD, Emeritus Professor, School of Medicine, University of New Mexico; Clinical Director, Child & Adolescent Services, Charter Hospital of Albuquerque; and Medical Director, Namaste Residential Treatment Center)*

Sexual Abuse and Residential Treatment, edited by Wander de C. Braga, MD, and Raymond Schimmer (Vol. 11, No. 1, 1994). *"Ideas are presented for assisting victims in dealing with past abuse and protecting them from future abuse in the facility." (Coalition Commentary [Illinois Coalition Against Sexual Assault])*

Milieu Therapy: Significant Issues and Innovative Applications, edited by Jerome M. Goldsmith, EdD, and Jacquelyn Sanders, PhD (Vol. 10, No. 3, 1993). *This tribute to Bruno Bettelheim illuminates continuing efforts to further understand the caring process and its impact upon healing and repair measures for disturbed children in residential care.*

Severely Disturbed Youngsters and the Parental Alliance, edited by Jacquelyn Sanders, PhD, and Barry L. Childress, MD (Vol. 9, No. 4, 1992). *"Establishes the importance of a therapeutic alliance with the parents of severely disturbed young people to improve the success of counseling." (Public Welfare)*

Crisis Intervention in Residential Treatment: The Clinical Innovations of Fritz Redl, edited by William C. Morse, PhD (Vol. 8, No. 4, 1991). *"Valuable in helping us set directions for continuing Redl's courageous trail-blazing work." (Reading [A Journal of Reviews and Commentary in Mental Health])*

Adolescent Suicide: Recognition, Treatment and Prevention, edited by Barry Garfinkel, MD, and Gordon Northrup, MD (Vol. 7, No. 1, 1990). *"Distills highly relevant information about the identification and treatment of suicidal adolescents into a pithy volume which will be highly accessible by all mental health professionals." (Norman E. Alessi, MD, Director, Child Diagnostic and Research Unit, The University of Michigan Medical Center)*

Psychoanalytic Approaches to the Very Troubled Child: Therapeutic Practice Innovations in Residential and Educational Settings, edited by Jacquelyn Sanders, PhD, and Barry M. Childress, MD (Vol. 6, No. 4, 1989). *"I find myself wanting to re-read the book–which I recommend for every professional library shelf, especially for directors of programs dealing with the management of residentially located disturbed youth." (Journal of American Association of Psychiatric Administrators)*

On Transitions from Group Care: Homeward Bound

Richard A. Epstein, Jr., MA
D. Patrick Zimmerman, PsyD
Editors

On Transitions from Group Care: Homeward Bound has been co-published simultaneously as *Residential Treatment for Children & Youth,* Volume 20, Number 2 2002.

The Haworth Press, Inc.
New York • London • Oxford

On Transitions from Group Care: Homeward Bound has been co-published simultaneously as *Residential Treatment for Children & Youth*™, Volume 20, Number 2 2002.

Cover design by Jennifer Gaska

Library of Congress Cataloging-in-Publication Data

On transitions from group care : homeward bound / Richard A. Epstein, D. Patrick Zimmerman, editors.
    p. cm.
    "Co-published simultaneously as Residential treatment for children & youth, volume 20, number 2, 2002."
    Includes bibliographical references and index.
    ISBN 0-7890-2054-8 (hard : alk. paper) – ISBN 0-7890-2055-6 (soft : alk. paper)
    1. Child psychotherapy–Residential treatment [DNLM: 1. Child Behavior Disorders–rehabilitation. 2. Adolescent. 3. Residential Treatment. 4. Social Adjustment. 5. Social Support. WS 460 O772 2004] I. Epstein, Richard A. MA. II. Zimmerman, D. Patrick, Psy.D. III. Residential treatment for children & youth.
RJ504.5.O5 2004
362.2′1′083–dc21

2003001519

Indexing, Abstracting & Website/Internet Coverage

This section provides you with a list of major indexing & abstracting services. That is to say, each service began covering this periodical during the year noted in the right column. Most Websites which are listed below have indicated that they will either post, disseminate, compile, archive, cite or alert their own Website users with research-based content from this work. (This list is as current as the copyright date of this publication.)

Special Bibliographic Notes related to special journal issues (separates) and indexing/abstracting:

- indexing/abstracting services in this list will also cover material in any "separate" that is co-published simultaneously with Haworth's special thematic journal issue or DocuSerial. Indexing/abstracting usually covers material at the article/chapter level.
- monographic co-editions are intended for either non-subscribers or libraries which intend to purchase a second copy for their circulating collections.
- monographic co-editions are reported to all jobbers/wholesalers/approval plans. The source journal is listed as the "series" to assist the prevention of duplicate purchasing in the same manner utilized for books-in-series.
- to facilitate user/access services all indexing/abstracting services are encouraged to utilize the co-indexing entry note indicated at the bottom of the first page of each article/chapter/contribution.
- this is intended to assist a library user of any reference tool (whether print, electronic, online, or CD-ROM) to locate the monographic version if the library has purchased this version but not a subscription to the source journal.
- individual articles/chapters in any Haworth publication are also available through the Haworth Document Delivery Service (HDDS).

On Transitions from Group Care: Homeward Bound

CONTENTS

ABOUT THE EDITORS

Richard A. Epstein, Jr., MA, received his master's degree from the University of Chicago, where he is currently a doctoral candidate in the Department of Psychology (Committee on Human Development). He is Program Manager at the Sonia Shankman Orthogenic School at the university and Managing Editor of *Residential Treatment for Children & Youth.*

D. Patrick Zimmerman, PsyD, is Director of Admissions and Psychotherapy Services at the Sonia Shankman Orthogenic School and Lecturer in the Department of Psychiatry at the University of Chicago. He is also a member of the Senior Associate Faculty of the Illinois School of Professional Psychology–Chicago. Dr. Zimmerman is a graduate of the Chicago Center for Psychoanalysis and serves as a member of its Board of Directors. He is currently Co-Editor of *Residential Treatment for Children & Youth.*

Foreword

Residential care and treatment of young people has a long and check-ered history. Any attempt to fully appreciate its nuances and complexi-ties is sure to fail. However, to ignore this mode of treatment as a part of the broader therapeutic options for children and adolescents would be a terrible mistake.

The history of residential treatment is complex because it encompasses a broad variety of settings that might include such diversity as prisons, or-phanages, therapeutic boarding schools and hospitals. This history in-cludes wonderful success stories, as well as tales of horror and abuse. And, of course, there is a remarkable lack of careful investigation into what works and what does not. However, even in the present day, it re-mains quite clear that there are children and adolescents who have prob-lems of sufficient magnitude that even the best, intensive, community-based interventions simply are not sufficient to protect the youth and pro-vide even a remote chance for even a moderately successful adaptation in the larger community.

Part of the problem of defining what treatment is "appropriate" for a given youth is that there has always been competition amongst the "help-ing professions" over which discipline or setting has "jurisdiction" over a particular problem domain (Abbott, 1988). The group care for children and adolescents is one area in which this competition comes to its fullest expression. Even a cursory look at the development of group or residen-tial care will show the "influences" of professionals from disciplines as diverse as psychiatry, education, psychoanalysis, social work and the clergy. Although contemporary views of psychiatry and psychology have had a large impact on current practice, there are many who have histori-cally influenced modern practice. One of the earlier practitioners who

[Haworth co-indexing entry note]: "Foreword." Leventhal, Bennett L. Co-published simultaneously in *Residential Treatment for Children & Youth* (The Haworth Press, Inc.) Vol. 20, No. 2, 2002, pp. xvii-xxiii; and: *On Transitions from Group Care: Homeward Bound* (ed: Richard A. Epstein, Jr., and D. Patrick Zimmerman) The Haworth Press, Inc., 2002, pp. xi-xvii. Single or multiple copies of this article are available for a fee from The Haworth Document Delivery Service [1-800-HAWORTH, 9:00 a.m. - 5:00 p.m. (EST). E-mail address: getinfo@haworthpressinc.com].

xi

tried to build a theoretical base for residential treatment was August Aichhorn in his work to create and operate an institution for delinquent boys in Oberhollabrunn, Austria, in 1917. His classical book, *Wayward Youth* (1925/1965), reported on one of the most touching experiments in humanity, his attempts to develop and provide psychological treatment for delinquent young people, as an alternative to the punitive atmosphere of threats, punishment, flogging and segregation typical of the existing reformatories of the time. Out of the shambles of a former refugee camp, Aichhorn immersed himself in creating a more benign treatment environment for incorrigible young people, adapting Freud's theories and techniques to his own rehabilitative efforts aimed at the personality structure of delinquents. This was a remarkable effort that somehow seems to have been forgotten as contemporary "correctional facilities" take a more punitive approach to very similar children.

A little more than twenty years after Aichorn, another historic effort to provide therapeutic group care for children was launched. Attending to a completely different type of child and seemingly different clinical problem associated with childhood trauma (but, was it so different?) Anna Freud recognized a special need for children impacted by the Nazi bombings in England that began in 1940. Concerned for both the physical safety and psychological security of young children exposed to this seemingly senseless violence, she worked with others to develop temporary shelters, or "war nurseries," to care for children experiencing the ravages of war. Initially developing temporary shelters in London for these children, she soon developed a more ambitious scheme involving comprehensive residential programs in Hampstead and in the countryside around London. Despite the urgency of the situation, Freud was careful to develop a theoretical framework in which she could develop programs. Not surprisingly, she turned, in part, to the work of Aichhorn concerning the impact of institutional care on the lives of children. To this she added her own psychoanalytic concepts and the educational framework developed by Montessori. This became a viable model for residential treatment that was widely praised and accepted.

Not content to just create programs, Anna Freud studied the results of her efforts and published them for the clinical world to consider. She largely used anecdotal and observational study of children residing in the war nurseries to share her knowledge and experiences, as basic empirical methods for this kind of work were simply not available at that time (Freud, 1941-45/1973). This work was covered in the 56 monthly reports over the time from February 1941, through December 1945. By the end of the war, it was apparent that the work of Freud and her colleagues might have applications not only in "war nurseries," but also for the more general care of children and adolescents in community-based and residential settings. Her work is worthy of contemporary consideration, as well. Freud thoughtfully addressed such questions as how to maintain contact with parents, psychological contagion within the residential group, and the relationship between children and their workers. Importantly, the "war nursery" writings provide observations on children's psychological reactions to witnessing the actual destruction of war while also describing different types of anxiety displayed by the children in the face of extraordinary stressors along with their most common defense and coping mechanisms. But, especially relevant, Freud and Burlingham offered a lengthy discussion of the advantages and disadvantages of residential care, especially in contrast to typical family-based care. While not definitive, this work suggests that there truly is a place for specifically planned and organized residential treatment for a carefully selected group of children.

The development of the concept of "milieu" by Fritz Redl and Bruno Bettelheim seemed to substantially add to notions about how to provide care for many types of patients but, above all, gave a name and framework for perhaps the most salient element of residential care. Building on the work of Aichhorn and Anna Freud, the notions of "milieu" and "milieu therapy" became essential elements in the work with troubled children and adolescents, particularly in urban areas of the United States. Others joined in developing these practices and concepts, including Rudolph Ekstein at the Southard School of the Menninger Clinic in Topeka, Kansas, and Redl and Wineman's work with delinquent boys at the Pioneer House.

The Pioneer House experiment was influenced in important respects by the research of Kurt Lewin and his colleagues at The University of Michigan's Research Center for Group Dynamics (1947/1951). As interpreted by Redl and Wineman (1951, 1952), Lewin's focus on the personally significant life-space, and the interplay of life-space and group process, provided a model for facilitating change in troubled young people who were experiencing personal disorganization and, as a result, were unable to live with others. Redl and Wineman sought to integrate the classical drive theory directed work with delinquent children first formulated by Aichhorn (1925/1965), with psychoanalytic ego psychology and educational models developed by Anna Freud, as well as the social psychology from the studies of Lewin and his colleagues. It was a bold attempt that still is still recognizable in contemporary residential and non-residential treatment programs.

Despite the current controversy about Bruno Bettelheim, there is much to be learned from his interest in the impact of environmental stressors on development and psychopathology and how this might inform treatment models. He seems to have been first inspired to consider this work by his personal experiences in the Nazi concentration camps. This initial work focused principally on the impact of stressors or trauma on the development of a sense of individuality. Reflecting on the power of the concentration camp to contribute to the destruction of personality (Bettelheim, 1943, 1960), Bettelheim recognized the power of the total environment to change behavior for good or ill. Accordingly, his therapeutic concern at the Orthogenic School of the University of Chicago was initially with the construction of a total treatment environment that would positively promote a capacity for mastery, a sense of integrity and ultimately a restored sense of individuality. Bettelheim's work was decidedly different from that of Redl that focused methods of behavioral control, techniques for therapeutic interview interventions in the milieu, and strategies for maintaining the structure or framework of the milieu, all for staff members. In short, Redl's focus was much more on the techniques for *management of group process* (including the elaboration of the concept of the "life-space interview") and understanding the effects of the group upon the individual. In contrast, at the Orthogenic School, the structure or framework of the milieu was assumed–it rested significantly upon the authoritative presence of an individual, in this case Bettelheim. As a result, many of Bettelheim's descriptions of the residential treatment program and milieu largely describe the rationale, structure and effects of an *already existent* cohesive well-organized, yet organizationally simple, therapeutic environment on the emotional process of rehabilitation. His work tended to emphasize anecdotal illustrations from highly detailed psychodynamic case material of individual students, rather than the specification of practical strategies or techniques for maintaining the stability of a therapeutic setting.

The extent to which Bettelheim shared in the tradition of the work done by Aichhorn and Redl is reflected in part by his early enthusiastic interest in the treatment of delinquent youth and in his belief in the potentially beneficial effects of milieu treatment for them (Bettelheim, 1955; Bettelheim and Sylvester, 1949a,b, 1950). However, over time, Bettelheim gradually shifted the major thrust of his work and writings away from delinquency and began to concentrate on the etiology and milieu treatment of schizophrenic children, as well as of a small group of autistic children (Bettelheim, 1955, 1967). Despite this change, the over-riding characteristics of Bettelheim's therapeutic milieu (irrespective of psychiatric diagnosis) emphasized that the specific treatment plan for each child should be an almost *unconditional gratification* of the child's basic needs, a secure and protective setting, and the selective provision of *carefully measured dosages of reality.*

Various iterations of the milieu models offered by Aichorn, A. Freud, Redl, Wineman, and Bettelheim enjoyed considerable popularity during the first two decades after the Second World War, with a number of other children's centers adopting the milieu treatment model (Trieschman, Whittaker, & Brendtro, 1969). In addition to the psychodynamic milieu approach, a number of other types of treatment milieu for troubled youth were developed subsequent to the early psychoanalytically based programs (Zimmerman, 1990). Some of those developments have included the "positive peer culture" model (Brendtro & Wasmund, 1989), behavioral therapy (Blase, Fixsen, Freeborn, & Jaeger, 1989), and Hobbs' residential psychoeducational approach (Lewis & Lewis, 1989).

So, why this lengthy focus on the development of residential treatment models? We certainly can learn from the past but, more importantly, we can see in the evolution of these treatment paradigms a changing understanding not only of child development and its variations, both normative and pathological, but also how treatment models changed in response to these emerging concepts. Of course, many of the struggles of our forbear were focused on developing models and dealing with basically qualitative issues that arose from the desire to deal with a variety of humanistic issues: (1) a wish to understand the character formation of anti-social young people, and to construct a benign environment for their rehabilitation; (2) the need to develop an understanding of early childhood developmental processes based upon observation, and to cast those processes within a general psychodynamic theory; (3) an attempt to provide a living environment for child victims of wartime trauma, and to understand the effects of ongoing environmental violence, separation from and permanent loss of family members upon their psychological functioning; (4) a better understanding of management techniques for impulsive, aggressive children; and (5) the expansion of our clinical knowledge to include a range of what had been previously considered to be untreatable disorders, including psychosis and autism.

The present landscape is decidedly different from that of our predecessors. First of all, there are new and dramatic treatments, pharmacologic and environmental that have dramatically altered the care and course of childhood onset psychiatric illness. Additionally, social and statutory pressures have changed the impetus behind treatment. These pressures include the Individuals with Disabilities Education Act (IDEA) that compels schools to provide appropriate education for all children, changes in the juvenile justice system, and monumental changes in funding for healthcare (Eist, 1997). Most of these forces are actually economic rather than clinical. As a result, there continues to be a lack of a coherent treatment model for all children, especially those who require carefully orchestrated transitions in and out of highly restricted care settings.

Our modern era has also seen a separation of psychiatry from its traditional relationship with psychoanalysis. Psychiatry has clearly integrated biological models, including psychopharmacology, with cognitive and cognitive-behavioral concepts and treatment techniques. With this has come a more medical model of group care that is more closely affiliated with the field of psychiatry than ever before. While there have been many changes in the group care of children and adolescents, one of the most dramatic differences may be shortening of lengths of stay. Still another has been the demand for empirically based treatments that are specific for a particular condition and have defined goals and endpoints. And finally, there is a specific insistence that residential care be integrated into a larger model of care, thus increasing the necessity of carefully designing appropriate transition plans and aftercare services.

As complex as the history might seem and as daunting are the challenges of the present, it is clear that the field has advanced. There are safe and effective residential treatments for children. And, there is still interest in thoughtfully improving these treatments, even in the face of the extraordinary pressures placed on facilities, clinicians and even the youths themselves. It is this growth, change and genuine progress that are the focus of the present volume. Herein lies a menu of reality coupled with the appealing notion that there is room for improvement, all in the context of a genuine, compassionate understanding and care of children, adolescents and their families when they most need it to face the challenges of human development gone awry. In this volume, Richard Epstein and Patrick Zimmerman have compiled a volume of studies that address the complexity of issues involved in transitions from group care back into life in the community. They use careful observation and empirical methods to teach us what is being done and help to set the agenda for next steps. It is illuminating and it is promising. Above all, this work shows that we have many opportunities to help our youth and their families, only to reinforce our obligation to do so, with the equity and effectiveness that we offer all children and families who suffer the pains of illness.

Bennett L. Leventhal, MD
Irving B. Harris Professor of Child and Adolescent Psychiatry
Professor of Psychiatry and Pediatrics
Director, Child and Adolescent Psychiatry
Director, Sonia Shankman Orthogenic School

REFERENCES

Abbott, A. (1988). *The System of Professions.* Chicago: The University of Chicago Press.

Aichhorn, A. (1925/1965). *Wayward Youth* (Trans. E. Bryant, J. Deming, M. O'Neil Hawkins, G. Mohr, E. Mohr, H. Ross, & H. Thun). New York: The Viking Press.

Bettelheim, B. (1943). Mass behavior in an extreme situation. *Journal of Abnormal and Social Psychology*, 38, pp. 417-452.

Bettelheim, B. (1955). *Truants from Life.* New York: The Free Press.

Bettelheim, B. (1960). *The Informed Heart.* New York: The Free Press.

Bettelheim, B. (1967). *The Empty Fortress.* New York: The Free Press.

Bettelheim, B. (1949a). Milieu therapy: Indications and illustrations. *Psychoanalytic Review*, 36, pp. 54-68.

Bettelheim, B. (1949b). Physical symptoms in emotionally disturbed children. *The Psychoanalytic Study of the Child*, 4, pp. 353-368. New York: International Universities Press.

Bettelheim, B. (1950). Delinquency and morality. *The Psychoanalytic Study of the Child*, 5, pp. 329-342. New York: International Universities Press.

Blase, K.A., Fixen, D.L., Freeborn, K., & Jaeger, D. (1989). The behavioral model. In R.D. Lyman, S. Prentice-Dunn, & S. Gabel (Eds.), *Residential and Inpatient Treatment of Children and Adolescents*, pp. 43-59. New York: Plenum Press.

Brendtro, L.K., & Wasmund, W. (1989). The peer culture model. In R.D. Lyman, S. Prentice-Dunn, & S. Gabel (Eds.), *Residential and Inpatient Treatment of Children and Adolescents*, pp. 81-96. New York: Plenum Press.

Eist, H.I. (1997). Managed care: Where did it come from? What does it do? How does it service? What can be done about it? *Psychoanalytic Inquiry*, 1997 Supplement, pp. 162-181.

Freud, A. (1941-45/1973). Monthly Reports to the Foster Parents' Plan for War Children, Inc., New York. In A. Freud, *The Writings of Anna Freud, Volume III, 1939-1945*, pp. 3-540. New York: International Universities Press.

Freud, A., & Burlingham, D. (1944/1973). Infants without families: The case for and against residential nurseries. In A. Freud, *The Writings of Anna Freud, Volume III, 1939-1945*, pp. 543-664. New York: International Universities Press.

Lewin, K. (1947/1951). Frontiers in group dynamics. In D. Cartwright (Ed.), *Field theory in Social Science*, pp. 87-129. New York: Harper and Brothers.

Lewis, W.W., & Lewis, B.L. (1989). The psychoeducational model: Cumberland House after 25 years. In R.D. Lyman, S. Prentice-Dunn, & S. Gabel (Eds.), *Residential and Inpatient Treatment of Children and Adolescents*, pp. 82-113. New York: Plenum Press.

Redl, F., & Wineman, D. (1951). *Children Who Hate.* Glencoe, IL: The Free Press.

Redl, F., & Wineman, D. (1952). *Controls from Within.* Glencoe, IL: The Free Press.

Trieschman, A., Whittaker, J., & Brendtro, L. (1969). *The Other 23 Hours: Child-care Work with Emotionally Disturbed Children.* Chicago: Aldine Publishing Company.

Zimmerman, D.P. (1990). Notes on the history of adolescent inpatient and residential treatment. *Adolescence*, 25(97), pp. 9-38.

Preface

Although the quality of the research literature on the outcomes of residential treatment for emotionally disturbed children and adolescents has been criticized for its lack of scientific rigor (Curry, 1991, 1995), that literature clearly suggests the importance of transition planning and the stability of the post-residential treatment discharge environment as important factors in determining the maintenance of treatment gains after discharge (Leichtman, Leichtman, Barber, & Neese, 2001). That suggestion, however, presents the provider of residential treatment services with several difficulties. First, transition planning and the stability of the post-residential treatment discharge environment are often in large measure factors that are beyond the control of the residential treatment program. Second, the limited resources of residential treatment centers often dictate that transition planning and ensuring the stability of post-residential discharge environments do not receive adequate attention (Whittaker, 2000). Third, there are simply limits to the availability of post-residential treatment discharge placement options, particularly given the current preference of public funding sources for family reunification.

The selections in this volume are devoted to helping answer the question of how providers of residential treatment services can promote more positive and successful transitions for the children in group care to less restrictive levels of care in other parts of the community in which they reside. In chapter one, Tim Lemmond and David Verhaagen discuss the development of a program designed to involve parents and caregivers in the residential treatment and transition process for sexually aggressive youth. In chapter two, Mary Peterson and Mark Scanlan discuss diagnosis and placement variables that affect the outcome of adolescents with behavior disorders in an outpatient mental health clinic. In chapter three,

[Haworth co-indexing entry note]: "Preface." Epstein, Richard A., Jr. Co-published simultaneously in *Residential Treatment for Children & Youth* (The Haworth Press, Inc.) Vol. 20, No. 2, 2002, pp. xxv-xxvi; and: *On Transitions from Group Care: Homeward Bound* (ed: Richard A. Epstein, Jr., and D. Patrick Zimmerman) The Haworth Press, Inc., 2002, pp. xix-xx. Single or multiple copies of this article are available for a fee from The Haworth Document Delivery Service [1-800-HAWORTH, 9:00 a.m. - 5:00 p.m. (EST). E-mail address: getinfo@haworthpressinc.com].

xix

Richard Knecht and Mary Hargrave discuss the development of a program at River Oaks Center for Children that is designed to redesign an existing residential treatment program to allow parents, caregivers, and the broader community a much more integral role in the child's residential treatment experience. In chapter four, Scott Dowling and his colleagues discuss the transitional living program at Bellefaire/JCB and present case studies of children who have participated, with both successful and unsuccessful outcomes, in their program. In chapter five, Patrick Zimmerman discusses the role of social skills training programs in facilitating successful transitions from residential treatment to the community.

We hope that this volume provides an opportunity for all practitioners engaged in providing quality residential treatment services to troubled youth to see how some colleagues are attempting to address the complex issues involved in providing quality transitional services to the young people in their care. That the provision of quality transitional services is necessary is unequivocal. The question of how to best incorporate transitional services into traditional residential treatment programs or to redesign those programs remains, however, an issue with which we all must continue to struggle.

Richard A. Epstein, Jr., MA

REFERENCES

Curry, J.F. (1991). Outcome research on residential treatment: Implications and suggested directions. *American Journal of Orthopsychiatry*, 61(3), 348-357.

Curry, J.F. (1995). The current status of research in residential treatment. *Residential Treatment for Children & Youth*, 12(3), 1-17.

Leichtman, M., Leichtman, M.L., Barber, C.C., and Neese, D.T. (2001). Effectiveness of intensive short-term residential treatment with severely disturbed adolescents. *American Journal of Orthopsychiatry*, 71(2), 227-235.

Whittaker. (2000). Reinventing residential childcare: An agenda for research and practice. *Residential Treatment for Children & Youth*, 17(3), 13-30.

Successful Transitions of Sexually Aggressive Youth from Secure Residential Treatment Settings to Less Secure Community Settings

Tim Lemmond, MA
David Verhaagen, PhD

SUMMARY. A major hurdle in the treatment of sexually aggressive youth (SAY) involves maintaining treatment gains achieved in secure residential settings during and following transitions to less secure residential settings. This article presents a philosophical framework for residential treatment programs that can guide policy and practice to achieve successful transitions. The approach emphasizes the importance of the secure residential program facilitating the SAY's family and non-family caretakers to achieve consensus on (1) what skills the SAY must develop to reduce risks of offense (treatment goals), (2) what situational and internal conditions produce higher risks (monitoring needs), and (3) what situational and internal conditions reduce risks (support needs). A framework for developing that consensus with primary caretakers at the time of admission is also described, and a specific curriculum designed to guide the development of a "Treatment Ally Team" while the SAY is in residential treatment is also presented. The Treatment Ally Team is an active part of the treatment process and continues to monitor and support

[Haworth co-indexing entry note]: "Successful Transitions of Sexually Aggressive Youth from Secure Residential Treatment Settings to Less Secure Community Settings." Lemmond, Tim, and David Verhaagen. Co-published simultaneously in *Residential Treatment for Children & Youth* (The Haworth Press, Inc.) Vol. 20, No. 2, 2002, pp. 1-13; and: *On Transitions from Group Care: Homeward Bound* (ed: Richard A. Epstein, Jr., and D. Patrick Zimmerman) The Haworth Press, Inc., 2002, pp. 1-13. Single or multiple copies of this article are available for a fee from The Haworth Document Delivery Service [1-800-HAWORTH, 9:00 a.m. - 5:00 p.m. (EST). E-mail address: getinfo@haworthpressinc.com].

the SAY during and after discharge. This model is seen as applicable to a variety of step-down placements including home, therapeutic foster care and non-secure community residential settings. *[Article copies available for a fee from The Haworth Document Delivery Service: 1-800-HAWORTH. E-mail address: <getinfo@haworthpressinc.com> Website: <http://www.HaworthPress.com> © 2002 by The Haworth Press, Inc. All rights reserved.]*

KEYWORDS. Residential treatment, transition planning, sexually aggressive youth

INTRODUCTION

Treating sexually aggressive youth (SAY) in residential treatment centers (RTCs) allows for intensive focus on treatment, strict control of the youth's environment, and protection for the community from further assaults. It is this last factor that is often central to the choice of residential treatment, rather than outpatient interventions. However, successful treatment does not just depend on gaining new skills while in a treatment milieu; it also depends on whether the youth is able to use these skills after returning to the community. Those community environments are necessarily much less controlled, less intensively focused on non-aggression and may include non-inhibiting or even provocative factors that contributed to the sexual aggression. The challenge of the RTC, therefore, is not only to have an effective treatment approach for the sexually aggressive youth, but also to help the youth utilize these skills successfully in the home community or in a less secure community placement. We suggest that the RTC be proactive in this regard. To do this, we believe the RTC's treatment model must address a number of functional issues related to the sexual aggression, while helping the youth's support system learn to promote this improved functioning in the home community, as well as to play a role in monitoring the youth's behavior after leaving the RTC.

It has become an accepted standard that residential programs for sexually aggressive youth should be highly structured and focus specifically on sexual aggression (Groth, Hobson, Lucey, & St. Pierre, 1981; Margolin, 1983; Ryan, Lane, Davis, & Isaac, 1987; Saunders & Awad, 1988). These programs generally are based on the notion that sexual offenses are the result of a "cycle" of cognitive, emotional, physiological, social and situational events which conclude in a sexual assault (Ryan et al., 1987; Morenz & Becker, 1995). Some programs approach this by emphasizing the interruption of deviant arousal through cognitive-behavioral techniques (Abel, Becker, & Cunningham-Rather, 1984; Becker & Kaplan, 1993). Others emphasize training the youth to learn the complex cycle leading up to abuse and also how to take corrective actions to avoid progressing along the path toward re-offense (Gray & Pithers, 1993).

Lemmond and Verhaagen (2002) have recommended that RTC's be more flexible in tailoring the treatment approach to the unique needs of a particular sexually aggressive youth along nine parameters that are significantly associated with sexual aggression: (1) sexual under-socialization, (2) past physical and sexual abuse, (3) deviant arousal, (4) rage, (5) substance abuse or dependence, (6) power/control, (7) trust, (8) sociopathy, and (9) family dysfunction. Because sexually aggressive youth vary widely on these parameters, Lemmond and Verhaagen (2002) further recommend assessing these parameters separately and designing individual treatment goals and interventions to build skills areas where deficits are identified. It is strongly emphasized that building the youth's unique array of skills in the identified deficit areas be the focus of treatment, rather than a single-focus model that assumes all sex offenders have the same deficits and the same needs. When expressed in terms of needed skills these areas are described as follows:

- Sexual Socialization
- Resolution of Past Physical and Sexual Abuse
- Deviant Arousal Management Skills
- Rage Control
- Sobriety
- Non-Abusive Personal Power
- Trust Skills
- Empathy and Respect for the Rights of Others
- Functional Family Relationships

As a youth progresses in the RTC, efforts are made to ensure that he/she has learned and practiced new skills and abilities to address the deficit areas that had been identified in the initial or subsequent assessments.

Consider, for example, the residential treatment of a 13-year-old boy who has a pattern of deviant arousal, combined with distorted thinking that allows him to violate the physical privacy of younger children and a history of being unsuccessful and rejected by same-age peers. A simplified description of the RTC's treatment goals might be to: (1) develop skills to manage the deviant arousal (e.g., identifying and avoiding high-risk circumstances, identifying and intervening in the early stage of the offense cycle), (2) develop increased emotional empathy for the victim and an understanding of why and how the sexual behavior with the victim was wrong and injurious, and (3) develop skills and abilities that will allow for more age-appropriate social success. After the youth has demonstrated the acquisition of these target skills and abilities, the challenge for the RTC becomes helping the youth learn to use these skills in the step-down environment (home or less-secure community placement), while maintaining some degree of security for the community and remaining available to help if problems occur. This is made even more complex if the youth's caretakers in the step-down environment don't understand the youth's unique needs. It is further complicated if the youth is discharged from the RTC before he has been able to practice these new skills and abilities in the step-down setting.

THE ROLE OF THE "TREATMENT ALLY TEAM"

The concept of "treatment allies" is a departure from traditional models of medical treatment. In the more traditional medical model, "treatment" is something done to the "patient" by trained professionals who possess special knowledge and skills. The "patient" is then "cured" by the activities of the professional and returns to the community without the affliction. With the concept of "treatment allies," non-professional (often family) support systems are engaged in the treatment process. The goal of this involvement is that they, too, may share in the professional's special knowledge so that they can monitor and support the youth's functioning in the community.

In the case of sexual aggression, the "special knowledge" involves an understanding that sexual aggression is often a habitual chain or cycle of feelings, decisions and behaviors that may have predictable triggers or "risk factors" and lead toward committing a sexual assault (Gray & Pithers, 1993; Way & Spieker, 1997). These risk factors may be internal factors such as certain emotional states, deviant sexual fantasies or states of intoxication. They may also be external situational factors such as being alone with potential victims. In addition, sexually aggressive persons are at more risk to act out when they begin to operate with certain flawed beliefs often called "thinking errors" (Gray & Pithers, 1993). These flawed beliefs may provide the youth with an internal, pseudo-logical justification to commit an act of victimization.

The treatment of sexually aggressive persons often must involve the client in learning about his or her own particular risk factors and the chain of internal and external events that could lead to sexual aggression. The goal of this aspect of treatment is to learn specific strategies that can disrupt the chain of behaviors early in the process to prevent the chain leading to an assault. This process is referred to as "relapse prevention" (Gray & Pithers, 1993). Family and non-family caretakers, potential caretakers, extended family members and others may become "treatment allies" when they, too, learn about the client's particular risk factors. These allies must also share in a detailed understanding of the corrective actions that the client has learned to use to break the risky chain of behavior well before an assault occurs. This knowledge can help them be in a position to remind, suggest, require and monitor the extent to which clients are behaving safely.

Professionals who object to having the family in a monitoring and supportive role often do so out of mistrust of family members. It is often reasoned that the client learned risky dynamics in the home and that release to the parents will simply undo the progress made in residential treatment. We contend that this is a strong argument for including the parents in the treatment early in the process, especially given that most clients will eventually return to their home environment regardless of what professionals decide. In many cases, family motivation to participate in learning about offender dynamics and to develop a relapse prevention plan exceeds the expectations of professionals (Lord & Barnes, 1996).

One way that parents and other potential caregivers can be prepared to perform support and monitoring functions early in the treatment process is by use of the treatment ally group. This is a formalized group facilitated by a therapist and consisting of those individuals who will potentially be caregivers in the youth's discharge environment. Using this inclusion criterion, the group may consist of family members, extended family members, para-professionals who will work with the young person after discharge, and virtually any other persons that occur to the group who could help the youth be successful if they knew his or her needs. The make-up of the team can change as additional persons are identified who could help with the young person's functioning.

THE TREATMENT ALLY TEAM GROUP CURRICULUM

The "Treatment Ally Team" group curriculum consists of three phases. The section that follows describes each of the phases, focusing specifically on the goals of each phase and the role of the group facilitator in helping the group meet those goals.

Phase One: "Forming and Establishing a Group Focus"

The goals of phase one are to form and establish a focus for the treatment ally team. Objectives in this phase include: (1) choosing members who will likely be in a caregiver, supervisory or support role for the youth after discharge, (2) bringing these individuals together to achieve a mutual understanding of the need to be "allies" to the youth's treatment, (3) forming relationships based on mutual respect and trust, and (4) obtaining commitment to long-term participation as an "ally" to the youth.

The role of the facilitator in this phase is to work towards developing a working team of individuals who will monitor and support the youth's functioning after discharge. The group facilitator may be the youth's primary therapist or another who has a clear understanding of the youth's individualized treatment process and needs. Potential team members should be identified and begin to meet as early as possible in the youth's treatment process. The facilitator should work closely with involved professionals and family members in selecting a core group of "allies" who will be necessary to help the youth be successful. Initially, the selection criteria should have much more to do with the person's role in the youth's life than that person's current state of understanding or belief about the young person's risk to commit assaults. It would be very unwise to exclude a parent, for example, who currently does not believe that the child committed an assault if this parent will be responsible for supervising the youth after discharge.

The facilitator should pay close attention to developing effective working relationships between team members. In the early stages of meeting, the facilitator should make sure that each team member introduces him- or herself, including name and role. The facilitator should also help individuals clarify their commitments to the process and their understandings of the goal. Depending on the anticipated length of residential treatment, the team may meet less frequently during the early stages (no less than every 6 weeks is recommended).

Special consideration should be given by the facilitator to forming good working relationships between family (often non-professionals) and human services professionals or criminal justice professionals. Family involvement is usually a primary necessity for the ultimate success of the youth. Family members must be made to feel welcomed, valued and involved in the process. Care should be taken to emphasize positives about the family, to avoid the use of professional jargon that may confuse the layperson and to avoid negative judgments about the family. The facilitator should help family members who do not believe that the assault occurred understand this denial as normal, and that working through it is a process. Separate family sessions, parent support materials (Gil, 1987) and disclosure sessions with the youth at the appropriate time can ultimately help family members work through the denial. At this early stage, however, the goal is to help family members keep an open mind, while reducing their defensiveness and excessive guilt.

Phase Two: "Planning Support, Monitoring"

The goals of phase two are to plan, support, and monitor the youth's needs. The objectives of this phase include: (1) understanding the youth's risk factors, (2) understanding the youth's strengths, (3) understanding the youth's support needs, and (4) developing a "Support and Monitoring Plan."

The role of the facilitator during this phase is to engage the Treatment Ally Team in a process parallel to the youth's treatment. As the youth learns about his/her own risks, takes responsibility for offenses, resolves trauma, learns arousal management, resolves trauma issues and other treatment activities, the ally team needs to be kept updated on the issues and should discuss them in terms of what it implies about discharge needs and timing. At times, it may be appropriate for the youth to attend the Treatment Ally Team meeting and update the team on treatment progress. Helping family members break through their denial can be greatly enhanced by a disclosure from the youth. Of course, the decision to do this type of activity and the timing is highly individualized.

The most important thing for the youth to do with the ally team is to educate them on what he/she has learned about individualized risk factors. These are the internal events (emotion, arousal, fantasies) and external events (behaviors, decisions, situations) that may lead towards sexual aggression. The facilitator starts this type of meeting by restating why each member is involved, reminding all that their role is to help the youth be successful after discharge, and encouraging all present to treat the information that the youth shares with confidentiality and respect.

The facilitator also helps the youth and team to co-define the strengths that the youth displays. These are the functional abilities that provide the bases for the positive alternative coping that the youth will use instead of sexual aggression. Additionally, the facilitator helps the group to decide and agree with the youth on the ways in which they can act to support and monitor the youth's use of strengths, rather than sexually aggressive or maladaptive coping skills. For example, a boy identifies in therapy that feeling unattractive and rejected by girls is risky because his anger can turn into rage and the urge to assault a female. He has also learned in treatment that there are other ways he can deal with feelings of rejection but that he also needs other ways to achieve peer acceptance that does not involve the approval of females. The treatment ally group can then apply themselves to creating opportunities for the boy to achieve this peer acceptance outside of residential treatment in a well-supervised way (monitored friendships, sports teams, other group peer activities). They will also know that when rejection does occur that this represents a high risk situation, and the youth will need to be encouraged to use the alternative coping strategies (talking to therapist, journaling, etc.)

As these individualized support and monitoring approaches take shape, it may be necessary to change the composition of the team so that supervising adults know what they should be watching for and what kind of supports are needed. In the example above, the boy may achieve peer acceptance by being involved in a church community service group. The team may decide to add the church group leader to the treatment ally group so that proper supervision and support can occur in that context. Also, the boy may have identified that when feeling rejected, he has in the past begun to isolate himself and use pornography to enhance rape fantasies. The team needs to be clear about how these patterns represent warning signs and identify a plan for communication and response if they are observed. The team may want to add an outpatient therapist knowledgeable about the youth's issues to the team. The response plan may involve communicating warning signs to this therapist for discussion in therapy and temporarily tightening supervision until they are successfully processed in therapy.

Due to legitimate concerns over confidentiality, some may resist involving others in the group. Gray and Pithers (1993), in their "Relapse Prevention Model," recommend involving a "core prevention group" that may involve immediate family, treatment provider, caseworker and/or probation officer. Then they suggest adding an expanding concentric circle representing distinct spheres of influence. They also recommend that decisions of whom to include in the outer spheres of influence be made by the members in the core group. The advantage of adding members later to the core treatment ally group is that those sharing confidential information about the youth are selected on a need-to-know basis. It is also important to remember and respect that the legal guardian of the youth (if he/she is not legally an adult) must approve all sharing of confidential information (unless otherwise ordered by the court). It is recommended that including new members be discussed completely in the Treatment Ally

Team working towards consensus, but that the legal guardian sign legitimate authorization documents before any such person is included.

The team needs also to plan and agree to report any additional sexually aggressive behavior. Not only is there legal "duty to report" if a child is victimized or at risk, the open agreement to report by all team members which has been approved by the legal guardian helps the youth be more vigilant and, ultimately, less likely to act out.

Phase Three: "Transition and Testing"

The goals of the Treatment Ally Team in phase three involve testing the plan that has been put into place, as well as the youth's readiness for transition to a less secure environment. Objectives during this phase include: (1) testing the monitoring and support plan, (2) fine tuning the plan as needed, and (3) transition facilitation of the team.

The role of the facilitator in this phase is to assess the treatment ally team's feelings about the completeness of and confidence in the plan, assure that plan is complete, and begin a transition. It is wise to consider a graduated transition rather than an abrupt discharge because it allows the treatment ally team and the client an opportunity to test and fine-tune the plan. Transitions consist of time-limited visits to the post-discharge environment. During these visits, the team members will practice the monitoring and support activities they had planned. After the visit, the team meets and discusses each member's observations. The facilitator should challenge the team to do more than just report problems or absence of problems. This is when team members must develop the important skill of noticing the youth using strengths as well.

Generally speaking, transition visits should be progressively lengthened and a discharge date set as the team gains confidence in their monitoring and support ability. In most cases, youth are on their best behavior during this phase as they try to prove that they are ready for freedom. If the youth acts-out during the transition, it is important for the team to consider what the acting-out means. In some cases, the acting-out means that the youth still does not have enough self-control, and more residential treatment may be indicated. But applying new skills in a new environment may very often not be done perfectly on the first try. So long as the acting out is caught early (before an assault occurs), it may turn into a valuable teaching situation. For this to be the case, the team monitoring and processing component must be in place.

Once the discharge has occurred, the team needs to continue as a functional unit. The facilitation of the team needs to be transferred to an existing team member for this to occur. In many cases, the outpatient therapist may play this role. However, it can also be successful if the caseworker, probation officer, parent or other team member takes on the role. What is most important is that someone take the responsibility for scheduling meetings, selecting a venue and keeping the group task oriented while meeting. It is also very useful for the facilitator to keep minutes of specific plans or agreements.

A BRIEF CASE EXAMPLE

Raymond is a 16-year-old, sexually aggressive client in a residential treatment program. He sexually assaulted a younger boy in his neighborhood by fondling while Raymond lived with his mother. Raymond's mother was a single parent at the time of the assault. He is in residential treatment to learn about his risk factors and to deal with a complex set of anger issues. He is also working on sobriety issues, since he was intoxicated at the time of the assault. The plan is for him to step-down into a Treatment Family (specialized foster care) Home in a neighborhood without young children. He is to begin home visits with his mother from the Treatment Family Home. In this case, Raymond's Treatment Ally Team originally involved his mother, his mother's live-in boyfriend, residential program treatment professionals and Raymond's juvenile probation officer. As this team learned about Raymond's specific risk factors, it was able to develop the discharge plan. The plan allowed Raymond both contact and involvement with the family, and an opportunity for Raymond to practice new skills in a more highly supervised treatment family home setting prior to returning home. Shortly before discharge, the treatment family home parents, the school counselor and outpatient therapist were also added to the group. Thus, a well-informed team of supports was ready to monitor and assist Raymond as he returned to the community. This group was already working and discussing Raymond's risk factors and treatment progress prior to his discharge. The group could easily continue in this well organized and functional way after discharge.

CONCLUSION:
PROGRAMMATIC GUIDELINES
FOR SUCCESSFUL TRANSITIONS

Although this article focused on how to make these transitions successful, we recommend that the following programmatic guiding principals (with associated policy and training) be central to the RTC's treatment model when dealing with sexually aggressive youth.

First, there must be early consensus on the target discharge environment. If both the youth and the treatment professionals have a "target discharge environment" in focus during the treatment process, it helps everyone remain focused on how the treatment relates to the youth's long-term goals. Even if the target discharge environment changes during the course of treatment, it can be very valuable in helping the focus of the program not stray into issues of superficial compliance and cooperation. Instead, both youth and treatment staff are challenged to explore how each new skill that is learned can work for the youth outside the RTC. From the youth's perspective, it can also be very helpful to focus him/her on the future of what can be accomplished through successful treatment. Those referring the youth for treatment should not develop a sense of complacency that the youth is "locked up." Rather, they must see placement in the RTC as a temporary measure that achieves short-term safety from assaults, but it does not relieve the larger issue of achieving successful community placement.

Second, the caregivers in the youth's discharge environment must understand the youth's particular risk factors and newly developed coping skills. Through treatment, the youth learns about his/her high-risk situations and develops functional alternatives to coping with these. These "high-risk situations" might be external situations (e.g., babysitting or visiting a playground unsupervised). The coping skills may include avoiding these situations, or otherwise using safeguards to lower risk (not going to the playground without a "safe" adult present). The high-risk circumstances might be "internal" (e.g., deviant fantasies or reversion to faulty beliefs which dis-inhibit acting-out). The caregiver needs to have a good working understanding of high-risk situations and the skills that the youth has learned to apply in each.

Third, the caregivers in the discharge environment must be prepared and enabled to support and monitor the youth's functioning in the discharge environment. If the RTC has a parallel focus helping the youth's future caregivers understand the particular risks and coping strategies, these caregivers can have the necessary knowledge to develop and implement a quality plan to support the use of these new skills after discharge and to monitor the extent to which the youth is choosing to monitor him/herself. The RTC is in a uniquely advantageous position during the course of treatment to educate and facilitate the team in transferring this information into an effective plan. Also, the youth may directly participate in this process by telling team members what is being learned as treatment progresses. This opens the door for later honest dialogue about the reality of the risks after the RTC is out of the picture.

Fourth, the youth must practice utilizing new coping skills in the designated discharge environment. Once the youth has demonstrated needed skills in the RTC and a plan has been developed for a team to monitor and support the youth's functioning, the youth needs to practice these skills in a safely monitored setting outside the RTC. This transition has the dual benefit of allowing the youth to practice the new skills in the target environment, as well as of giving the team of caregivers an opportunity to test the monitoring and support plan that has been developed.

Finally, any unforeseen difficulties and issues should be identified and dealt with while the support of the residential environment is still in place. If during this transition phase an unforeseen difficulty arises, it is not a treatment failure, it is instead a sign that more work is needed. It may be that a new aspect of the youth's functional deficits comes to light during the transition. During this time, it may also be discovered that the team of caregivers are not communicating as expected, or that the monitoring plan has an unanticipated flaw in it. These types of circumstances can be managed by extending the discharge date, while using the added time to more adequately address the problem.

REFERENCES

Abel, G. G., Becker, J. V., & Cunningham-Rather, J. (1984). Complications, Consent, and Cognitions in Sex Between Children and Adults. *International Journal of Law and Psychiatry*, 7, 89-103.

Becker, J. V. & Kaplan, M. S. (1993). In Barbaree, H. E., Marshall, W. L. and Hudson, S. M. (Eds.) The Juvenile Sex Offender. New York, NY, Guilford Press pp. 264-277.

Gil, E. (1987). *Children Who Molest: A Guide for Parents of Young Sex Offenders.* Walnut Creek, CA: Launch Press.

Gray A. & Pithers, W. (1993). Relapse Prevention with Sexually Aggressive Adolescents and Children: Expanding Treatment and Supervision. In Barbaree, H.E., Marshall, W. L., and Hudson, S. M. (Eds.) *The Juvenile Sex Offender*. New York, NY, Guilford Press pp. 203-224.

Groth, A. N., Hobson, W. F., Lucey, K. P., & St. Pierre, J. (1981). Juvenile sexual offenders: Guidelines for treatment. *International Journal of Offender Therapy and Comparative Criminology*, 25, 265-275.

Lemmond, T. & Verhaagen, D. (2002). *Residential Treatment of Sexually Aggressive Youth*. Westport, Connecticut: Greenwood Press.

Lord, A. & Barnes, C. (1996). Family Liaison Work With Adolescents in a Sex Offender Treatment Programme. *Journal of Sexual Aggression*, 2(2), 112–121.

Margolin, L. (1983). A Treatment Model for the Adolescent Sex Offender. *Journal of Offender Counseling, Services and Rehabilitation,* 8, 1-12.

Morenz, B. & Becker, J. (1995). The treatment of youthful sexual offenders. *Applied and Preventative Psychology* 4: 241-256.

Ryan, G., Lane, S., Davis, J., & Isaac, C. (1987). Juvenile sex offenders: Development and Correction. *Child Abuse and Neglect,* 11, 385-395.

Saunders, E. B. & Awad, G. A. (1988). Assessment, Management and Treatment Planning for Male Adolescent Sexual Offenders. *American Journal of Orthopsychiatry,* 60, 460-465.

Way, I. F. & Spieker, S. D. (1997). Cycle of Offense: A Framework for Treating Adolescent Sexual Offenders. Notre Dame, Indiana: Jalice Press.

BIOGRAPHICAL NOTES

Tim Lemmond, MA, is a licensed psychological associate and nationally certified psychologist (MA, Western Carolina University). He is the former clinical director of a child abuse treatment center and specialist in working with sexually aggressive youth and adults, as well as victims of various childhood traumas. Tim has consulted with numerous mental health agencies in several states to teach community-based service delivery approaches for seriously disturbed adolescents and their families. He has been involved as a consultant on several residential program design projects in secure residential, independent living group-homes and specialized foster care settings. He is co-author (with Dr. Verhaagen) of *Residential Treatment for Sexually Aggressive Youth* (2002, Greenwood Press).

David Verhaagen, PhD, is a licensed psychologist (PhD, UNC-Chapel Hill) and the former Clinical Director of three mental health agencies that serve children and their families. He has consulted with numerous residential programs around the country. He is on the Board of Directors for the Children's Law Center and has served on various committees, including Mecklenburg County's Serious Habitual Offender, Juvenile Sexual Offender, and Post-Adoption Services committees. He is the co-author of three books, including a recent comprehensive guide to residential treatment for sexually aggressive youth. He has made over 90 professional presentations in the past nine years. He is currently the director of Southeast Psychological Services in Charlotte.

Correspondence may be sent to Tim Lemmond, 1515 Mockingbird Lane, Suite 902, Charlotte, NC 28209.

Diagnosis and Placement Variables Affecting the Outcome of Adolescents with Behavioral Disorders

Mary Peterson, PhD
Mark Scanlan, MD

SUMMARY. The treatment of adolescents with behavior disorders represents significant challenges. This article reviews some of the most effective behavioral and pharmacological treatments identified in the research. The study used outcome data from a residential treatment program to identify variables that predicted level of functioning post-discharge. Significant variables included diagnosis (mood vs. behavior disorder spectrum), co-morbidity and discharge placement. *[Article copies available for a fee from The Haworth Document Delivery Service: 1-800-HAWORTH. E-mail address: <getinfo@haworthpressinc.com> Website: <http://www.HaworthPress.com> © 2002 by The Haworth Press, Inc. All rights reserved.]*

KEYWORDS. Behavior disorders, mood disorders, outcome variables

INTRODUCTION

Adolescents with a diagnosis of conduct disorder represent a significant challenge in assessment and treatment. A multi-agency task force recently reviewed the data from adolescent referrals in the Medicaid

[Haworth co-indexing entry note]: "Diagnosis and Placement Variables Affecting the Outcome of Adolescents with Behavioral Disorders." Peterson, Mary, and Mark Scanlan. Co-published simultaneously in *Residential Treatment for Children & Youth* (The Haworth Press, Inc.) Vol. 20, No. 2, 2002, pp. 15-23; and: *On Transitions from Group Care: Homeward Bound* (ed: Richard A. Epstein, Jr., and D. Patrick Zimmerman) The Haworth Press, Inc., 2002, pp. 15-23. Single or multiple copies of this article are available for a fee from The Haworth Document Delivery Service [1-800-HAWORTH, 9:00 a.m. - 5:00 p.m. (EST). E-mail address: getinfo@haworthpressinc.com].

15

population in the state of Nebraska. Data revealed that the larger spectrum of conduct disorder behaviors accounted for approximately 50% of clinical referrals. These referrals utilized approximately 63% of the treatment dollars spent during 1999 (Lyons & Leon, 1999). Most of these referrals were for a level of care that necessitated residential treatment.

Conduct Disorder (CD) is a diagnosis that is easy to make and difficult to treat. In contrast to DSM-III R criteria, DSM-IV criteria allow for subtyping CD according to age of onset (before or after age 10) and severity (mild, moderate or severe.) The age based amendment reflects empirical findings that show a different co-morbidity profile between childhood-v. adolescent-onset CD. Also, children with childhood-onset CD seem to have a greater frequency of neuropsychiatric disorders, including low IQ, ADHD, aggression and familial clustering of externalizing disorders.

There are many studies documenting the extensive comorbidities found with CD (Loeber & Keenan, 1994; Pfeffer, Klerman, Hurt, Kakuma, Peskin, & Siefker, 1993; Soltys, Kashani, Dandoy, & Vaidya, 1992). Of the externalizing disorders, ADHD is a common comorbid condition, along with ODD and substance abuse. Among internalizing disorders, mood and anxiety disorders are common. Some studies also show a high frequency of PTSD in confined adolescent males (Burton, Foy, Bwanuasi, & Johnson, 1994; Steiner, Williams, Benton-Hardy, Kohler, & Duxbury, 1998).

A thorough multi-dimensional assessment across situations and reporters is necessary to accurately identify CD in adolescence. Self-report may minimize the problems and omit events that show disturbance (Bank, Duncan, Patterson, & Reid, 1993; Kazdin, 1992; Luiselli, 1991). A detailed and comprehensive neuropsychiatric evaluation should be completed with close attention to the medical history, including accidents, injuries and corresponding deficits and dysfunction. There is wide agreement in the field that the best treatment of CD is multi-modal which includes the medical, cognitive, behavioral, educational, family and environmental vulnerabilities of each child.

The literature demonstrates a positive response for comorbid ADHD symptoms using CNS stimulants. In addition to their effectiveness, they are well studied, effective and safe when appropriately monitored and show substantial short term beneficial effects (American Academy of Child and Adolescent Psychiatry, 1991, 1997; Hinshaw, Buhrmester, & Heller, 1989; Hinshaw, Heller, & McHale, 1992). There are additional medication options based on the comorbid condition or specific target symptoms. These include neuroleptics for paranoia, psychotic ideation and aggression, although side-effects can potentially outweigh benefits

(Aman, Marks, Turbott, 1991; Campbell, Gonzalez, Ernst, 1992; Campbell, Gonzalez, & Silva, 1993). Antidepressants, particularly the SSRI's, are used to target depressive and anxiety disorders along with impulsivity. Clonidine and quanfacine are used for hyperarousal symptoms, commonly in tandem with stimulants.

Anti-convulsants or mood stabilizers are used for bipolar disorder and states of mood lability or severe impulsivity. Sedative and anxiolytics (especially benzodiazepines and antihistamines) generally showed limited usefulness and their problematic side-effects on memory and cognition, along with abuse potential, precluded any regular therapeutic usage (Vieselmann, Yaylayan, Weller, 1993).

In looking at the behavioral treatment, it is important to note the research findings regarding the treatment of adolescents with CD. Dishion, McCord and Poulin (1999) highlight the problems related to the iatrogenic effects that occur in peer-group interventions. Their longitudinal research showed that the "deviancy training" which happens in long-term treatment group settings, increases adolescent problem behavior and negative life-time outcomes. Other research has supported the negative influence of deviant peers on the psychosocial development of adolescents (Patterson, 1993; Elliott, Huizinga & Ageton, 1985).

The research has identified the most effective interventions to treat the adolescents with a conduct disorder. One of the most effective alternatives identified in the research (Kazdin & Weisz, 1998) appears to be Multi-Systemic Therapy (MST). MST develops interventions and support within the family and uses the family/systemic strengths as treatment "levers" to help move and shape the adolescent's behavior. Other empirically supported treatments include cognitive-problem-solving skills (Crick & Dodge, 1994; Spivack & Shure, 1982) and Parent Management Training (Graziano & Diament, 1992). The cognitive problem-solving skills training (PSST) approach trains youth to identify appropriate, pro-social ways to achieve their goals, as well as to identify potential negative consequences to their behavior. The Parent Management Training (PMT) helps parents to attend to appropriate behavior while responding directly and consistently to disruptive or deviant behavior. All three of these treatment approaches (MST; PSST and PMT) have been documented as effective and appropriate treatments for children and adolescents with conduct disorders (Kazdin & Weisz, 1998). Importantly, none of these treatments involve the aggregation of youth with conduct disorder.

Residential treatment level of care is often considered essential for high-risk adolescents. Residential treatment is required for those adolescents who represent significant risk to themselves or others and who cannot be maintained in a community setting. Many of these adolescents have a diagnosis within the behavior disorder spectrum. The adolescents within this spectrum present a unique challenge, because the group environment of a residential program may be at odds with the concept of family and home interventions that have been identified as successful strategies in the research.

METHODS

Following the review of the literature we decided to conduct an outcome study that analyzed the outcome of our population according to the variables suggested in the literature, including diagnosis, comorbidity and living environment. We were interested in learning whether post-discharge success (as measured by GAF) was influenced by the variable of diagnosis type (conduct disorder spectrum vs. mood disorder spectrum), comorbidity (number of diagnoses on discharge) or discharge placement (home, foster care, treatment group home).

Participants

The subject population included 37 males drawn randomly from the total population of 92 males, who participated in the Residential Treatment Center (RTC) program at Regional West Medical Center (RWMC) in Scottsbluff, Nebraska during the time period between June, 1999, to January, 2001. The RTC program at RWMC is a small, 8-bed program in a rural community in western Nebraska. The program uses a combination of positive peer-culture and a structured behavior modification program.

The subject population had a wide variety of diagnoses: 17 subjects had primary mood disorder diagnoses and 20 subjects had primary behavior disorder diagnoses. Comorbidity was high: only 2 subjects had a single diagnosis; 15 subjects had two diagnoses; 11 had three diagnoses; 4 had four diagnoses; and 5 had five diagnoses.

Discharge placements varied along the continuum of care and included 12 subjects returning to their homes, 13 to a level of care consistent with treatment group homes, 7 to levels of care consistent with therapeutic foster care, and 5 to other residential treatment centers.

Procedures

Data collection involved contacting the caregivers of a cross-section of our treatment population (n = 37) to identify the adolescent's level of functioning at 6 to 12 months post-discharge. A variety of people performed the role of caregiver and included parents, case-managers, therapists, and other program staff according to discharge placement. The contact was made by telephone by either a clinical psychologist or master's degree level intern using the same protocol. The length of time post-discharge varied between 6 and 12 months with a mean of 8.1 months post-discharge.

Measures

The diagnoses were made by the Medical Director of the RTC program at RWMC after an initial 2-week assessment and observation period, with input from a multi-disciplinary team. Diagnoses that had "rule-out" status were not included. The Global Assessment of Functioning score was used to assess overall functioning. This measure provided a "common language" across providers to assess functioning in a wide variety of domains, including home, school and social. The protocol prompted the caregiver to consider functioning across all domains.

RESULTS

We found that the three variables of diagnosis type (conduct disorder spectrum vs. mood disorder spectrum), comorbidity and discharge placement all contributed to a significant part of the variance when predicting GAF at post discharge follow-up. When we compared the data between those residents with a conduct disorder spectrum diagnosis with those given a mood disorder spectrum diagnosis, we found a significant difference in their success rates ($F(2, 35) = 22.06$ p < .0001). Adolescents with a primary mood disorder were functioning at a significantly higher level than those with a primary behavior disorder.

Our data also indicated significant negative correlation between comorbidity and post discharge success (Figure 1). Again, the effect was greater for those adolescents with the conduct disorder spectrum ($F = (1,35)$ 26.63 < .0001.) Discharge placement was the third variable that contributed a significant part of the GAF variance on follow-up. The majority of our residents were discharged to treatment group home level of care. However, those residents that were discharged to either home or treatment foster care had significantly higher GAF scores at follow-up. When we analyzed all variables in a simultaneous regression, the three variables accounted for 63% of the variance of GAF outcome ($R = .815$,

FIGURE 1. GAF Scores as a Function of Number of Comorbid Diagnoses

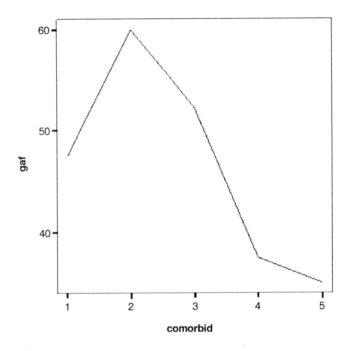

$R^2 = .664$, SE = 7.53. Diagnosis B = -9.75, SE = 2.75; Discharge placement B = -2.97, SE = 1.10; Comorbid B = -4.55, SE 1.29).

DISCUSSION

In discussing our results, we expected that those residents with a primary mood disorder would function at a higher level than those with primary conduct disorder spectrum diagnosis. The results of the follow-up data indicated that this was an accurate prediction. Adolescents with conduct disorder spectrum may be more treatment resistant, evoke negative responses from peers and caregivers and negatively affect their level of functioning. We also predicted that comorbidity would negatively affect adjustment. Our results also supported that predication. The multiple diagnoses and complex symptom picture of many of our adolescents interfered with their ability to acquire the behavioral skills and emotion management that is required in step-down placements.

However, the effect that discharge placement had on the functioning level of these adolescents was unexpected. Adolescents with conduct disorder spectrum diagnoses showed a lower level of functioning when placed in group home environments than in foster or family-home environments.

The data from our small program appears to be consistent with the review of the literature that indicates that a home environment is the best placement in which treatment can occur for an adolescent with a primary or secondary diagnosis of conduct disorder. The reason for that success may be the lack of "deviancy training" or it may be the development of wrap-around services that are anchored to a home environment. However, there is a secondary benefit to RTC programs, as they then are able to treat their adolescent populations without the effect of "deviancy training" by the conduct disordered adolescents. Thus, the axiom of "there's no place like home" is often true for many reasons.

REFERENCES

American Academy of Child and Adolescent Psychiatry. (1997). Practice parameters for the assessment and treatment of children, adolescents, and adults with attention-deficit/hyperactivity disorder. *Journal of American Academy of Child Adolescent Psychiatry, 36*(suppl), 85S-121S.

Aman, M.G., Marks, R.E., Turbott, S.H. et al. (1991). Methylphenidate and thioridazine in the treatment of intellectually subaverage children: Effects on cognitive-motor performance. *Journal of the American Academy of Child & Adolescent Psychiatry, 30*(5), 816-824.

Bank, L., Duncan, T., Patterson, G., & Reid, J. (1993). Parent and teacher ratings in the assessment and prediction of antisocial and delinquent behaviors. *Journal of Personality, 61,* 693-709.

Burton, D., Foy, D., Bwanuasi, C., & Johnson, J. (1994). The relationship between traumatic exposure and post-traumatic stress symptoms in male juvenile offenders. *Journal of Trauma Stress, 7,* 83-93.

Campbell, M., Gonzalez, N.M., Ernst, M. et al. (1993). Antipsychotics (neuroleptics). In J.S. Werry and M.G. Aman (Eds.), *Practitioners Guide to Psychoactive Drugs for Children and Adolescents.* New York: Plenum Press, 269-296.

Campbell, M., Gonzalez, N.M., & Silva, R.R. (1992). The pharmacologic treatment of conduct disorders and rage outbursts. *Psychiatric Clinics of North America, 15,* 69-85.

Crick, N.R., & Dodge, K.A. (1994). A review and reformulation of social information processing mechanisms in children's social adjustment. *Psychological Bulletin, 115,* 74-101.

Dishion, T.J., & McCord, J. (1999). When interventions harm. *American Psychologist, 54*(9), 755-764.

Elliott, D., Huizinga, D., & Ageton, S. (1985). *Explaining Delinquency and Drug Use.* Beverly Hills, CA: Sage.

Graziano, A.M., & Diament, D.M. (1992). Parent behavioral training: An examination of the paradigm. *Behavior Modification,* 16, 3-38.

Hinshaw, S., Buhrmester, D., & Heller, T. (1989). Anger control in response to verbal provocation: Effects of stimulant medication for boys with ADHD. *Journal Abnormal Child Psychology,* 17, 393-407.

Hinshaw, S., Heller, T., & McHale, J. (1992). Covert antisocial behaviors in boys with attention-deficit hyperactivity disorder: External validation and effects of methylphenidate. *Journal of Consulting and Clinical Psychology,* 60, 264-271.

Kazdin, A. (1992). Child and adolescent dysfunction and paths toward maladjustment: Targets for intervention. *Clinical Psychology Review,* 12, 795-817.

Kazdin, A.E., & Weisz, J.R. (1998). Identifying and developing empirically supported child and adolescent treatments. *Journal of Consulting and Clinical Psychology,* 66(1), 19-36.

Loeber, R., & Keenan, K. (1994b). Interaction between conduct disorder and its comorbid conditions: Effects of age and gender. *Clinical Psychology Review,* 14, 497-523.

Luiselli, J. (1991). Assessment-derived treatment of children's disruptive behavior disorders. *Behavior Modification,* 15, 294-309.

Lyons, J.S., & Leon, S.C. (1999). Children and Adolescents in Residential Treatment in Nebraska, Report to Value Options. In a report of the Mental Health Services and Policy Program, Institute for Health Services Research & Policy Studies. Chicago.

Patterson, G.R. (1993). Orderly change in a stable world: The antisocial trait as a chimera. *Journal of Consulting and Clinical Psychology,* 61, 911-918.

Pfeffer, C., Klerman, G., Hurt, S., Kakuma, T., Peskin, J., & Siefker, C. (1993). Suicidal children grown-up: Rates and psychosocial risk factors for suicide attempts during follow-up. *Journal of American Academy Child and Adolescent Psychiatry,* 32, 106-113.

Soltys, S., Kashani, J., Dandoy, A., & Vaidya, A. (1992). Comorbidity for disruptive behavior disorders in psychiatrically hospitalized children. *Child Psychiatry Human Development,* 23, 87-98.

Spivack, G., & Shure, M.B. (1982). The cognition of social adjustment: Interpersonal cognitive problem solving thinking. In B.B. Lahey & A. E. Kazdin (Eds.), *Advances in Clinical Child Psychology,* 5, New York: Plenum, 323-372.

Steiner, H., Williams, S.E., Benton-Hardy, L., Kohler, M., & Duxbury, E. (1997b). Violent crime paths in incarcerated juveniles: Psychological, environmental, and biological factors. In A. Raine, D. Farrington, P. Brennan, and S.A. Mednick (Eds.), *Biosocial Bases of Violence.* New York: Plenum, 325-328.

Vieselmann, J.O., Yaylayan, S., Weller, E.B. et al. (1993). Antidysthymic drugs (antidepressants and antimanics). In J.S. Werry and M.G. Aman (Eds.), *Practitioners Guide to Psychoactive Drugs for Children and Adolescents.* New York: Plenum Press, 1993, 239-268.

BIOGRAPHICAL NOTES

Mary Peterson, PhD, is a clinical psychologist and Clinical Coordinator for the Behavioral Health Center at Regional West Medical Center. She received her undergraduate and master's degrees from the University of Cincinnati and her doctoral degree from the California School of Professional Psychology.

Mark Scanlan, MD, is a board certified child and adolescent psychiatrist and Medical Director for the Behavioral Health Center at Regional West Medical Center. He is a graduate of the University of Kansas School of Medicine and completed his psychiatry residency at LomaLinda University Medical Center.

Correspondence may be sent to Mary Peterson, Partners in Behavioral Health, 2 West 42nd Street, Suite 3200, Scottsbluff, NE 69361.

Familyworks:
Integrating Family
in Residential Treatment

Richard Knecht, MS
Mary C. Hargrave, PhD

SUMMARY. Residential treatment for children and youth has been attacked for its failure to demonstrate a consistently positive impact on the lives of its clients. This paper describes one agency's efforts toward incorporating current research on "what works" to make residential treatment effective and to actively engage families in the process. *[Article copies available for a fee from The Haworth Document Delivery Service: 1-800-HAWORTH. E-mail address: <getinfo@haworthpressinc.com> Website: <http://www.HaworthPress.com> © 2002 by The Haworth Press, Inc. All rights reserved.]*

KEYWORDS. Residential treatment, out of home care, family therapy, wraparound services, mental health

INTRODUCTION

In recent years, residential treatment for troubled children and adolescents has come under attack for its high cost and its inability to clearly demonstrate effectiveness as a treatment intervention (Curry, 1991). One of the most unequivocal findings suggested in the research literature, however, is that the post-residential treatment discharge environment

---

[Haworth co-indexing entry note]: "Familyworks: Integrating Family in Residential Treatment." Knecht, Richard, and Mary C. Hargrave. Co-published simultaneously in *Residential Treatment for Children & Youth* (The Haworth Press, Inc.) Vol. 20, No. 2, 2002, pp. 25-35; and: *On Transitions from Group Care: Homeward Bound* (ed: Richard A. Epstein, Jr., and D. Patrick Zimmerman) The Haworth Press, Inc., 2002, pp. 25-35. Single or multiple copies of this article are available for a fee from The Haworth Document Delivery Service [1-800-HAWORTH, 9:00 a.m. - 5:00 p.m. (EST). E-mail address: getinfo@haworthpressinc.com].

may be one of the strongest predictors of the maintenance of treatment gains made by young people during residential treatment (Whittaker, 2001). As Whittaker (2001) states, "The cumulative findings of a number of outcome studies dating back to the 1960s seem to point to the critical role that family and community support factors play in determining post placement adjustment of children returning from residential care" (p. 177).

Although it may seem obvious that post-discharge factors such as family involvement and community support are important to the maintenance of treatment gains made during residential treatment, many residential treatment programs do not actively involve the family and community. Whittaker (1980) has noted that poorly planned and/or poorly managed family reunification efforts often leave children and families vulnerable to rejection and failure upon discharge and reunification. The more active facilitation of family and community involvement in the process of residential treatment may create a new generation of residential treatment programs that can better prepare for the troubled young person's transition to a life outside the institution—one that can create and sustain improvement, that is more cost-effective, and that represents a valuable addition to the "system of care" for any troubled young person.

As mentioned earlier, there is research to support the integration of family and community into the residential treatment process. Landsman, Groza, Tyler, and Malone (2001) report that a model of intensive, family-based residential treatment was more successful than traditional residential treatment in producing positive outcomes. Two important aspects of the family-based residential program were increased family visiting and shorter lengths of stay in residence. Stage (1999) found that children whose families attended family therapy were more likely to be discharged to less restrictive settings. Sunseri (2001) found that children who were visited frequently while in care were 5.7 times more likely to complete treatment than children with less frequent visitation. Additionally, children who went on home visits were also more likely to complete the program. Taub, Tighe, and Burchard (2001) report that empowered parents with children who have serious mental health problems, although not in residential treatment, report greater positive change in their children's externalizing behavior problems over time. In a review of outcome research on residential treatment, Curry (1991) cited several sources supporting the suggestion that good post-residential adjustment is associated with aftercare and "the need to work with the child and family for extensive periods of time, only some of it within residential treatment" (p. 352). In a study of post-discharge adjustment from Project Re-Ed programs, family and school data were more predictive of maintenance of gains than other variables, suggesting that intervention with the family and community was most favorable to positive outcome (Lewis, 1988). In a 1995 study of outcomes from psychiatric hospitalization, Parmelee, Cohen, Nemil, Best, Cassell, and Dyson (1995) found that living with a family member at the time of hospitalization and the family's participation in treatment planning during hospitalization were the most influential predictors of positive outcome.

The current paper will describe the planning and development of the River Oak Center for Children "Familyworks" program. The River Oak Center for Children is located in Sacramento, California. It is a multi-service provider of psychiatric-level residential services to children between the ages of 5 and 12 years. Approximately 60 children are served annually with presenting issues similar to those of other residential centers across the nation: severe emotional disabilities, learning problems, complex medical histories and frequent psychiatric hospitalizations. Children in the River Oak program are in need of significant mental health treatment and allied social services and are often at risk for life-long institutionalization. Their caregivers have also experienced frustration and lack of success as they have entered into and progressed through the mental health/special education/child welfare systems.

The Familyworks program is supported through a partnership with the Sacramento County, California, Department of Health and Human Assistance and represents the River Oak's effort to encourage caregivers to join with and participate in the planning and delivery of services to their children. The program offers parents the opportunity to participate in a variety of traditional program components: parenting classes, traditional family therapy, parents' support groups, parent partnership/advocacy, and in-home services. The goal of all component activities is to bridge the gap that exists for children and families attempting family reunification at this level of care. Over and above this more traditional menu of services, the unique aspect of Familyworks is its strong emphasis on caregiver participation within the residential treatment milieu, and its efforts to connect the child and family to their home community during and after the child's residential placement.

Since the inception of the Familyworks program in November 1999, approximately 18 families have participated in its unique effort to integrate family into residential treatment process. Increasing numbers of parents are expressing a desire to receive these specialized services. Children without obvious family resources are given a new way to connect with foster parents and greater support to reunite with kinship resources. Without exception, caregivers express profound optimism and regard for the service and the inroads it has provided for their family toward either reunification or a lower level of care.

THE DEVELOPMENT AND PLANNING
OF THE FAMILYWORKS PROGRAM

River Oaks had traditionally involved parents through the provision of supervised visitation, along with family therapy and parenting groups. Parent involvement and integration into aftercare services, however, was hampered by a lack of funding and prevalent "silo" thinking in mental health programming. We had long believed that more intensive and better parent-centered services were vital to the long-term success of our clients, but had not been able to systematically address the problem of how to provide such services.

Our executive management team convened an advisory council to address how our residential program could address the issue of providing family-centered services and to develop a plan to create such services. The advisory council identified better involvement of the residential treatment center in its external community, treatment team integration, and improved communication between service components as ancillary, but integral parts of providing family-centered services. Following the lead of the advisory council, the residential leadership team held a retreat to determine which resources would need to be created and what resources already existed within the agency to facilitate a change to becoming truly family-centered.

The principal obstacle was, not surprisingly, financial, and additional funding was necessary to create the network of services that would be needed. In the fall of 1999, negotiations were begun with the Sacramento County Division of Mental Health to fund services that would make it possible for parents and other permanent caregivers to be included in the residential treatment process (e.g., the Familyworks program). In addition, funding was designed so that it would be possible for staff from the center to go into the parent's homes on weekend visits or to community events to facilitate the transfer of learning from the center to community settings such as scouting or athletic teams.

With the personnel and other resources obtained via this contract, the agency hired clinical, program and parent advocacy staff to create an intensive family-centered program, with a full continuum of parent-centered interventions. One master's level clinician, one bachelor's level staff member, activity assistants, and an experienced consumer advocate were recruited and trained. Added to the existing agency services (supervised visitation and limited milieu involvement) was a continuum which included a 6-week orientation for the family to the residential treatment experience, participation by parents in the education and after-school programs, intensive family therapy continuing through aftercare, family advocacy supports, and the ability to support the family in its natural environment. Underscoring all of these program changes was an ideological shift toward caregiver-friendly service delivery. The significant adjustment required for all staff to become caregiver friendly was profound. (See Table A for a list of the family-centered services offered by the Familyworks program.)

At the same time, the agency was able to participate in an innovative "wraparound" program designed for children coming out of high levels of residential care. Wraparound services provided the aftercare components necessary for success after discharge from a residential treatment program. The need to integrate this community-based effort into the changes in residential culture was key to making the complete transition to a new way of conceptualizing residential treatment.

CHANGING THE SERVICES PROVIDED AND "RE-TOOLING" THE MILIEU CULTURE

All managers were trained and oriented to see parents as active, vital decision-makers regarding their child's care. Program leadership mod-

TABLE A. Family Centered Services

➤   Staff Supported Home Visitations
➤   Family Education
➤   Parent's Support Group
➤   Structured Family Activities
➤   Parent Advocacy
➤   Family Therapy
➤   Inclusion in Milieu Activities
➤   Child/Family Team Meetings

eled this new "attitude" at every moment, establishing an expectation that direct service staff would begin to view parents as capable, willing partners. Much of this change in organizational perspective came about by use of family-centered, empowering language that was free of parental condemnation. (See Table B for a list of the changes in institutional language and ways of thinking.) A variety of team meetings became the primary forum to verbally reinforce the changes. The impact of inclusion of family members in all treatment-planning functions crystallized these changes. The family advocacy services utilized a paid former consumer of services to further challenge the staff to see parents as active, concerned and capable partners.

TABLE B. Language Paradigm Shift

Old Concepts/Language	New Concepts/Language
Treatment Team Meeting	Child & Family Team Meeting
Problem identification	Needs identification
Complaining	Verbally expressive/able to state own needs
Controlling	Managing
Uninvolved	Private
"Nosey"	Stays informed/interested in child
Enmeshed	Enthusiastic, dedicated, committed to family
Nags and complains	Shares concerns/assertive
Dependent	Open to help
Obsessive	Vigilant
Stubborn	Committed
Adamant	Empowered
User/taker	Resourceful
Secretive	Protective
Child fixing and returning	Family support
No parent contact during adjustment phase	Continuous contact
Parent in the lobby	Parents everywhere
Home visits strictly rationed	Home visits supported by staff presence
Home visits contingent on child's behavior	Home visits essential to the program
Home a distant memory	Home integrated into everyone's thinking
Uncover the past	Move to a better future
Caretakers responsible for problems	Caretakers are key to the future

In order to hasten the paradigm shift, the Family Advocate and Familyworks social worker worked together to build bridges to parents who would otherwise have stayed distant from the treatment team. These were parents who perceived themselves as having been blamed by the system at some earlier date for their child's problems. From failure to improve during outpatient care to seeing their children removed from lower levels of care due to the severity of the children's difficulties, experience with the system and prior providers had been very demoralizing and engendering of loss of hope. Parents embraced the team of professionals more readily when they saw and understood that the staff exists not to keep them from their child, but to create the bridge for their child to return home. An expectation on the part of staff that parents would participate created a strong statement about the role of the parents in their child's recovery and in the future adaptation of their children.

Under this model, the residential childcare workers interacted with, mentored, modeled, redirected, reframed, and interpreted the possible meanings of the child's behavior for the child's parents. A review of milieu policies and procedures was necessary to support the presence of caregivers in the milieu. The result of the revisions of such residential treatment center routines was that parents are invited into the residence and, under clearly established guidelines, may be present with their child at various times throughout the day. It is this latter change that presented the greatest challenge to the residential treatment center–initiating the provision of new services was one thing, but changing milieu policy, undoing old ways of interacting with caregivers and creating a new milieu culture, was another.

With the job at hand identified, there were many changes that needed to take place. The following represents a rough chronology of the organization's effort to make the changes outlined above:

1. In July 1999, a contract was negotiated with Sacramento County Mental Health to fund a structured day rehabilitation program for residents and their caregivers.
2. In August 1999, the treatment model was reworked and we began to open the residential culture to caregivers as equal partners in the treatment process. One aspect of this "reworking" involved inviting parents to Child and Family Team Meetings so that they could be a part of the treatment planning process. The invitations involved other changes, such as an increased flexibility of scheduling. Another as-

pect of this "reworking" was the rewriting of our consent forms for services so as to have them reflect, reinforce, and emphasize the critical role of caregiver involvement in all services. Associated with the two previously mentioned changes was the redesigning of our treatment plan to reflect a strength-based, family-centered language and process, rather than the deficit-driven model that calls for intervention at the level of the affected individual alone.

3. In March 2000, we hired a social worker whose primary responsibility was to focus on enhancing caregiver connectedness and involvement. We also created a model of caregiver education, caregiver support, family treatment, and after-school program involvement. The after-school programs were recreation-based programs held during the work week in which caregiver involvement was encouraged.

4. In May of 2000, we hired a Family Advocate whose qualifications included being an ex-consumer (e.g., "experienced" parent) to engage in full-time advocacy work, networking with caregivers and professionals on the residential treatment team.

5. In October 2000, we changed the name of our residential programs to "Family Residential" services to better reflect our focus on involving caregivers and the families of our children in their treatment process.

6. In November 2000, we rewrote our caregiver orientation handbook so that it would more accurately reflect our commitment to better involve caregivers throughout the residential treatment process. This task involved rewriting our clinical policies and procedures to more accurately reflect our new emphasis on involving caregivers in their child's treatment at all phases including intake, visitation, and treatment planning.

7. In January 2001, we provided strength-based, caregiver-centered treatment planning training, combined with the continual and consistent didactic training of staff on how to work with and involve parents in the residential treatment process.

8. In February 2001, we established dedicated "wrap-around" services to help create or identify potential family, kin, or foster-based placements for those of our children who would become ready for discharge to step-down environments.

CASE STUDY

Marc was an 11-year-old Caucasian male who had spent about 10 months in the residential program when the family was introduced to

Familyworks. His mother and father had struggled with substance abuse, difficulty securing housing and a loss of hope. Placement workers gave the family little chance of successful reunification, because of the mother's history of substance abuse, the father's unstable work history, and challenges in engagement of county placement workers. Marc had a long history of placements and a general decline in his ability to function at home and in school.

The parents joined with the family advocate who was able to share her story and encourage the family to engage more actively in efforts to reunify with Marc. They attended the support group and family therapy, where they successfully learned new strategies for managing Marc's often-challenging behaviors. These were also supported at home. The Family Advocate accompanied the mother on job finding, connected her to food bank resources and assisted her in obtaining housing. The father was supported in job retraining, from seasonal construction to full-time truck driving. The family was successful in engaging with the county system to demonstrate their changes successfully to the courts and have now reunified with their son. Support from the wraparound service team was implemented prior to discharge for the post-residential plan.

CHALLENGES AND OUTCOMES

Staff who have successfully transitioned through these changes are more than repaid for their efforts as they find work with the families and children much more rewarding and successful. Turning the work upside down from negatives, however clinically stated, to positives requires constant attention. Individuals trained in psychopathological approaches to human behavior, who have not also experienced the power of regeneration of hope, can return to language and behavior patterns with families that have not been associated with success in the past.

One serious challenge to family-centered residential care is the fact that not all of the children come to the agency with family resources. The detective work involved with locating kinship resources or other connected people is intense and cannot be left to the old "discharge planning" mode. Pairing children with family resources in a milieu with those who are looking for those resources recapitulates a painful truth of abandonment and loss for children who are alone. Additionally, agencies often find themselves receiving referrals for placement from a desperate public system looking for a "bed." Explaining the family component of the pro-

TABLE C. Family Residential Program Average Length of Stay (in Months)

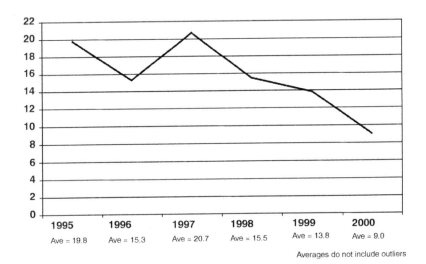

| 1995 | 1996 | 1997 | 1998 | 1999 | 2000 |
| Ave = 19.8 | Ave = 15.3 | Ave = 20.7 | Ave = 15.5 | Ave = 13.8 | Ave = 9.0 |

Averages do not include outliers

gram's philosophy can be a barrier to referrals but is never a barrier to successful outcomes.

The overall success of this paradigm shift can be seen in Table C, which depicts the average length of stay in our residential treatment program. The decline in length of stay from 14 months to 9 months after the implementation of the family residential program suggests that, at least in terms of decreasing the average length of stay in our residential treatment program, our Familyworks program has been a successful one. It may be that involving caregivers and families in the residential treatment of their child in a residential treatment program that offers a welcoming and supportive milieu coupled with aftercare services may lead to a strongly positive impact on children's lives.

REFERENCES

Curry, J.F. (1991). Outcome research on residential treatment: Implications and suggested directions. *American Journal of Orthopsychiatry*, 61 (3), 348-357.

Landsman, M.L., Groza, V., Tyler, M., and Malone, K. (2001). Outcomes from family-centered residential treatment. *Child Welfare, LXXX*, (3), 351-379.

Lewis, W.W. (1988). The role of ecological variables in residential treatment. *Behavioral Disorders*, 13, 98-107.

Parmelee, D.X., Cohen, R., Nemil, M., Best, A.M., Cassell, S., & Dyson, F. (1995). Children and adolescents discharged from public psychiatric hospitals: Evaluation and outcome in a continuum of care. *Journal of Child and Family Studies*, 4 (1), 43-55.

Stage, S.A. (1999). Predicting adolescents' discharge status following residential treatment. *Residential Treatment for Children & Youth*, 16, 37-57.

Sunseri, P. (2001). The prediction of unplanned discharge from residential treatment. Unpublished paper.

Taub, J., Tighe, T.A., & Burchard, J. (2001). The effects of parent empowerment on adjustment for children receiving comprehensive mental health services. *Children's Services: Social Policy, Research and Practice*, 4 (3), 103-122.

Whittaker, J.K. (1981). Family involvement in residential treatment: A support system for parents. In A. Maluccio & P. Sinanogh (Eds.), *The Challenge of Partnership: Working with Parents of Children in Foster Care*. CWLA Press: Washington DC.

Whittaker, J.K. (2001). What works in residential childcare and treatment: Partnerships with families. In M. Kluger, G. Alexander, & P. Curtis (Eds.), *What Works in Child Welfare*. CWLA Press: Washington DC.

BIOGRAPHICAL NOTES

Richard Knecht, MS, is Senior Vice-President of Clinical Operations at River Oak Center for Children. He has been affiliated with River Oak since September of 1997. Prior to joining River Oak, he worked as a social worker for a foster family agency and was C.O.O. of a large psychiatric hospital in Salt Lake City, Utah. In addition, he was former adjunct faculty at Utah Valley State College and Brigham Young University. He holds an MS in Counseling from California State University, Sacramento.

Mary C. Hargrave, PhD, is President and Chief Executive Officer at River Oak Center for Children. She is a 1967 honors graduate of California State University, Sacramento. She received her PhD from the University of Washington, Seattle, in 1972. She completed her post-doctoral work at Lackland Air Force Base in Texas. After working in residential and day treatment programs in Texas and Oregon, Dr. Hargrave joined River Oak in 1985.

Support for this project was provided through a partnership with the Sacramento County, California, Department of Health and Human Assistance.

Correspondence may be sent to Richard Knecht, River Oak Center for Children, 4330 Auburn Boulevard, Suite 2000, Sacramento, CA 95841.

The Bellefaire/JCB
Transitional Living Program:
A Program Description
and Preliminary Report of Outcome

Scott Dowling, MD
Suellen Saunders, MSSA, LISW
Cathy Marcus, LSW
Evan Langholt, MSSA, LISW
J. Ashby, MSSA, LISW

SUMMARY. The research literature on the outcomes of the residential treatment of emotionally disturbed children and adolescents suggests the need for residential treatment programs to prepare their clients for their eventual transitions back into the community. The current paper describes the Transitional Living Program of Bellefaire/JCB and presents a preliminary report of that program's client outcome. Descriptive statistics and case studies are used in the discussion of program outcome. *[Article copies available for a fee from The Haworth Document Delivery Service: 1-800-HAWORTH. E-mail address: <getinfo@haworthpressinc.com> Website: <http://www.HaworthPress.com> © 2002 by The Haworth Press, Inc. All rights reserved.]*

KEYWORDS. Residential treatment, transition planning, transitional living programs, adolescents

---

[Haworth co-indexing entry note]: "The Bellefaire/JCB Transitional Living Program: A Program Description and Preliminary Report of Outcome." Dowling, Scott et al. Co-published simultaneously in *Residential Treatment for Children & Youth* (The Haworth Press, Inc.) Vol. 20, No. 2, 2002, pp. 37-50; and: *On Transitions from Group Care: Homeward Bound* (ed: Richard A. Epstein, Jr., and D. Patrick Zimmerman) The Haworth Press, Inc., 2002, pp. 37-50. Single or multiple copies of this article are available for a fee from The Haworth Document Delivery Service [1-800-HAWORTH, 9:00 a.m. - 5:00 p.m. (EST). E-mail address: getinfo@haworthpressinc.com].

INTRODUCTION

One of the most consistent findings reported in the residential treat-ment outcome research literature is that although most emotionally dis-turbed children and adolescents improve during the course of their residential treatment, in-treatment improvement is not strongly predic-tive of outcome at follow-up (Curry, 1991, 1995; Leichtman, Leichtman, Barber, & Neese, 2001). This finding has led many reviewers of the resi-dential treatment outcome research literature to conclude that one of the most important things providers of residential treatment services can do for their clients is actively work to plan their eventual transition back to living in the community (e.g., Durkin & Durkin, 1975; Curry, 1991, 1995; Leichtman et al., 2001).

At Bellefaire/JCB we have developed a Transitional Living Program to help our clients develop the independent living skills that will be nec-essary for their eventual transitions back to living in the community to be successful. In the paper that follows, we will describe the setting of the Bellefaire residential program, describe our Transitional Living Program using case studies where appropriate, and present a preliminary report of that program's client outcome.

The Residential Programs at Bellefaire/JCB

Bellefaire/JCB is a large social service agency for children and fami-lies in the Cleveland, Ohio area, and is strongly supported by the Jewish Welfare Federation of Cleveland and the United Way. Bellefaire is a resi-dential treatment center for emotionally disturbed children and adoles-cents. The residential treatment center draws upon the extensive network of services available through the generosity of the Jewish community of Cleveland.

Bellefaire is located on a 32-acre campus in the midst of a middle-class neighborhood in suburban Cleveland. Bellefaire was originally founded in 1868 as a center for the care of Jewish children from the mid-western states who were orphaned during the United States Civil War. Following World War II and under the leadership of Dr. Morris Mayer, who is gen-erally regarded as one of the founders of residential treatment in the United States, Bellefaire became a well-known residential treatment cen-ter for emotionally disturbed children and adolescents.

At that time, treatment was provided under the supervision of psycho-analysts and included cottage-based milieu therapy, individual psycho-therapy, and educational treatment at the on-campus Bellefaire School.

Dr. Mayer expanded the services of Bellefaire to include a daycare center, foster care, group home care, and adoption services. Bellefaire has continued to evolve after Dr. Mayer's death in 1977. Currently, under the direction of Adam Jacobs, Ph.D., Bellefaire/JCB also provides outpatient psychotherapy, partial hospitalization, intensive inpatient treatment, and the Transitional Living Program. The extent of the services offered by Bellefaire/JCB can be judged by the fact that in 1999, more than 4,000 children, youth, and families were served.

The Bellefaire/JCB Transitional Living Program

The Bellefaire/JCB Transitional Living Program was developed in 1994 to provide emotionally disturbed adolescents with the ability to develop basic competence in dealing with the realities of day-to-day living. It was our hope that such a program would help our clients make more successful transitions into their adult lives in the community.

The Transitional Living Program seeks to assist its adolescent clients in meeting the central developmental requirement of late adolescence and young adulthood–namely, that of making the transition from a state of adolescent dependence to a degree of independence consonant with their continuing physical, intellectual, financial, and mental limitations. Fundamental to this transition is that the adolescent acquire a respectful sense of self and others, not as an abstract goal, but as a living, practical reality of the adolescent's daily experience. Every detail of planning and intervention in our program is geared towards fostering an awareness of personal responsibility and toward developing an awareness of the adolescents' varied relationships with family and friends (both adult and child), in the cottage, at work, and in the community.

The practical reality of education, work, family, and day-to-day relationships in the cottage and in the neighborhood in which the adolescent lives are the means through which this fundamental awareness is achieved. A corollary of these goals and this philosophy is that both youth and staff are accorded respect consistent with their place in the community and with their capabilities. Respect for clients begins with attribution of both meaningful responsibilities and rights as a young adult within the limits of personal capability. Authority, structure and discipline are the responsibility of staff who present unequivocal and individualized expectations and express them with clarity and vigor. Honesty, consideration for others, freedom to speak and to feel are among the responsibilities of both clients and staff. There is active discussion, confrontation, and consequence for behavior in all aspects of the adolescent's life. There is no restraint or seclusion. It is in this framework that we approach the issue of developing independent living skills, not as isolated techniques but as practical realities, through which an inner persisting awareness of self and others and of one's place in the world can take place.

Case Study 1: A Treatment Failure

Jim was 18 years old and had spent most of the previous six years of his life in psychiatric hospitals and closed-unit residential placements. Between placements there were intervals at home with his socially and financially privileged family. At these times, he regularly became involved in drugs and alcohol as part of a longstanding battle with his parents. His anger towards and resentment of his parents were veiled by an outward behavioral compliance and obedience. He had a strong sense of derisive entitlement. He did not, or perhaps could not, view the Bellefaire/JCB Transitional Living Program as any sort of opportunity for individual development and initiative. He persistently resorted to his usual patterns of deception, drug use, and undermining of community goals. Although many of these characteristics were present with other, more successful clients, Jim, over a period of six months, had not formed respectful relationships with staff or other clients and was discharged due to his repeated drug use.

The Transitional Living Program involves residential, educational, and psychotherapeutic components. The Transitional Living Program cottage is a self-contained unit with individual rooms for ten older adolescents, a large living-room area, a laundry, a kitchen, a telephone room, and three staff offices. Each adolescent's room is set up as an "efficiency apartment" and equipped with basic furniture and a small refrigerator. Personal arrangement of and additions to the furniture, as well as decoration of the room, are strongly encouraged. Radios and televisions are allowed in each room as a privilege earned by showing respect for self and others and are usually paid for out of the adolescent's own savings. The additional furniture and appliances are viewed as "starters" for the independent apartment the adolescent is eventually expected to achieve. Pagers and cellular phones are not allowed. Three evening meals are provided each week by Bellefaire, all other meals are prepared by each individual adolescent with the assistance of staff members.

The cottage is co-educational, and supervision is provided by a cottage manager, two cottage supervisors, and seven child-care workers. Staffing patterns are varied throughout the day to meet client needs. Each young person has a child-care worker assigned to him or her, but all staff work with all adolescents as necessity requires. The adolescent's "prime" worker is responsible for daily discussion with his or her client and for taking care of routine administrative details. All workers are, in a real sense, available to youth. Staffing strength varies with the number of youth in the cottage at any given time. The child-care workers are all college graduates, often with bachelor's degrees in psychology or social work, but usually do not have previous experience in residential child-care. All receive active on-the-job training and supervision, particularly in the skills of intervention with defiant, teasing, testing, and seductive adolescents. The two cottage supervisors are present during the day and serve as models for the child-care workers. They are also actively involved with the child-care workers in the more difficult situations of confrontation, intervention, interpretation and emotional support for the adolescents. They deal with the more complex administrative issues such as coordination, planning and meetings with county workers, probation officers, other officers of the court, police, school administrators, vocational programs, health care professionals, and, most importantly, with family members. The cottage supervisors or the cottage manager handles most such issues. There are, in addition, multiple opportunities for supervision, consultation, and additional education for all staff members with the cottage psychiatrist and with Bellefaire's supportive and administrative staff. Psychiatric, pediatric, nursing support, and psychiatric interventions (including medications and hospitalization) are available at all times.

Case Study 2: Dealing with the Family

Bill, an older adolescent with an unusual pattern of depression, severe suicide attempts with probable brain damage, cognitive disability, repeated psychiatric hospitalizations and institutionalization, is a striking example of how our clients often have a strong sense of attachment with what can only be considered a dysfunctional family. Bill's mother was a committed cocaine addict who organized her life and her family towards the continuation of her cocaine addiction. She taught Bill and her two older sons to steal for her. She alienated them from their father in order to maintain control over them. She opposed all efforts to help them as attempts to "meddle with her rights."

Bill had conflictual feelings about the "good life" he led in residential care as compared to his two brothers, who were incarcerated, and to his mother, who shuffled between crack houses. These feelings contributed to his persistent depression and his impulsive, but nevertheless quite severe, suicide attempts. Bill worked hard in the Transitional Living Program, but was then caught in what, for him, was an agonizing conflict between saving money to provide for himself or giving his money to his mother to help meet her insistent demands.

Program staff intervened to discuss with Bill's mother the effect that her demands was having on him, but to no avail. Ultimately, staff initiated contact with Bill's father, helped Bill work through his derisive feelings towards his father, and assisted them in forming a relationship in which the father could provide Bill with the supervision and support that Bill needed when he left our program. This relationship helped protect him from his mother, and Bill is no longer as severely depressed, is working to get ahead in school in spite of his cognitive limitations, and lives with his father.

The vehicle through which the milieu program is organized is a system of "phases" and "stages." The phases track the child's progress from the time of admission through to discharge. There are six phases: initial, beginning, intermediate, advanced, final and ultimate. Each phase is divided into "levels" and the child must accomplish a variety of tasks before moving on to the next level and phase. The tasks that comprise the levels include developing skills such as: budgeting/banking, meal preparation, cleaning/maintenance, employment/unemployment experience, health/hygiene, personal transportation, time management, education, and other responsibilities. The five "stages" list increasing responsibilities and privileges corresponding to the first five phases. An inability to complete phase requirements or to live within the responsibilities and privileges of the corresponding stage means retention at that level. A gross disruption of the program such as an AWOL or serious imposition on another resident reduces the young person to the initial phase. He or she can, however, quickly return to the previously achieved phase. Thus, the young person does not need to redo all the requirements from initial to advanced phase to return to their previous level of privilege and responsibility.

The key to this program is that the various phase items are the vehicles for discussion between adolescent and staff; they are NOT simply tasks that are "ticked off" with a new phase as the reward. Vulnerabilities, fears, attitudes, past experiences and special skills are revealed as the child is expected to become increasingly independent in making meal plans; learning about and using public transportation; thinking about, earning, saving, planning and spending money; participating with others in the care and cleaning of his living area; recognizing their view of themselves as a wage earner now and in the future; dealing with job applications and interviews, employers, fellow workers, and customers; recognizing the special needs of their body; and learning how to manage time. Underlying all discussions is the place of relationships–with themselves, friends, adults (staff), and, most fundamentally, with family. The effort is made, over time, to help them see how those relationships and their reactions to them have affected their ability to function well, to make choices, to do what they say and believe they wish to do.

The Stages provide an outline of expectations to which both the adolescent and responsible adult caretaker may refer. Curfews are set up, plans for visiting family and friends are made, shopping and entertainment are allowed within stated requirements for informing caretakers and keeping in touch should there be a change of plans. The youth is expected to keep contact; the responsible adult is expected to be a source of safety and oversight. We believe this unvarying adult commitment models and strengthens the internalization of self-control and self-esteem. Sustaining this commitment is the task of close supervision, modeling and community values.

Supplementing the above components of the program are regular house meetings in which positives about each resident are shared and cottage issues discussed. Discussion groups on such topics as sexuality (including contraception and protection from STD), women's issues, and employment are scheduled regularly as are group recreational activities such as weekly trips to the local library, attendance at sporting events, trips to the local Jewish Community Center for basketball and swimming and so on. Throughout all group activities, specific performance (e.g., winning, speaking more, or being more clever) is accepted but not specially rewarded, while consideration of others, self-awareness, and honesty of action and expression are strongly emphasized.

We would like to describe the use of phases and stages in one component of the milieu program in more detail, the approach to food, as it typifies much else in the actual day-to-day running of the program. Tuesday night is designated as shopping night, and all residents go as a group with a childcare worker to a local grocery store. They are free to use their $40 weekly food allowance for food items of their choice with two restrictions: food items from four food groups must be purchased and not more than $10 can be spent on snacks. Although some residents have worked in food stores or fast food restaurants, almost without exception the boys and girls in this program have never planned or shopped for meals and have no idea what to buy beyond a wish for snack food. Plans are made and budgets reviewed with the responsible childcare worker. Still, like so much else, the resident approaches the task with defensive bravado and an outward air of "get out of my way." In the Initial Phase, during the first week in the program, the resident accompanies others to the grocery store to "learn the ropes." They have a tour of the kitchen and learn how to operate and clean its various appliances. They learn the rules of operation of the appliances and use of the kitchen. In the Beginning Phase (after the first week), they prepare and must stay within a budget at the store, plan simple meals for each day with prepared foods, and clean up dishes, pots and pans and the dining area after each meal. In the Intermediate Phase, they learn food groups and must prepare meals from at least three groups. They learn how to choose, freeze, thaw, prepare and clean up meat dishes. In the Advanced Phase, they must show an ability to follow a recipe, plan and prepare a four-course meal for two, and prepare a meal with leftovers, learning how to store and protect the leftovers against spoilage. In the Final Phase, the resident demonstrates an ability to plan and eat nutritiously and prepares a farewell meal for the cottage, complete with proper place settings. In the Ultimate Phase, they plan for and buy needed dishes and cooking materials for their independent living apartment. They review and demonstrate knowledge of care and maintenance of kitchen appliances.

Case Study 3: Overeating and Obesity

Jill is a 17-year-old female who was admitted with diagnoses of Bipolar Disorder, Oppositional Defiant Disorder, and Mild-to-Moderate Retardation. Her clinical records indicated that she was impulsive, aggressive, and sexually promiscuous. She had been institutionalized throughout her adolescence. In fact, Jill was big, loud, and obscene, but also a "whiner" who sometimes threw temper tantrums like a much younger child. Her age-inappropriate, almost childlike, behaviors were her principal means of interacting with others. She was a sloppy overeater who would literally gorge herself with ice cream whenever it was available. Her first trip into the broader community was to the grocery and provided an early entry into observations with her about the intolerability of her behavior prior to admission. As staff and other clients got to know Jill, they realized that she was capable of interacting with others in a more age-appropriate manner. As her provocative behaviors drew a smaller and smaller audience, she became able to plan meals, behave at the grocery, and generally interact with others and around food in an appropriate manner.

It takes little imagination to grasp the multitude of opportunities and pitfalls, which this set of requirements entails. Often a lifetime of scattered, unplanned and nutritionally ambiguous eating comes to the fore as the resident battles against the worker's observations about taking good care of himself/herself and of community property, the value and enjoyment of different foods, the social value of sharing a meal and of mutual food preparation. Unfamiliar foods are tried for the first time. Inevitable comparisons with food at home come up. Pots and pans will be left for others to clean up, and how this is handled contributes strongly to the quality of relationship between staff and youth. It is important to realize that the final decision rests with the young person about his or her actual food purchases, although staff members are not silent about the choices made. A few weeks of little else but Hot Pockets, macaroni and cheese, minute steaks, potato chips and soft drinks usually gives way, under group pressure and awareness that others are eating interesting things, to a more rational and varied diet. There is pleasure in preparing fried chicken or lasagna. Those who wish to lose weight but stock up on ice cream and cookies are given the freedom to do so, but the issue enters into focused private discussions with staff intended to encourage self-examination. The skills of food-choice and food storage and preparation come not through dictate or an external formula, but rather through identification, modeling, insistence on safety, and a measure of freedom from past restrictions through discussion with staff.

The remainder of this paper will present a preliminary report of the outcomes of the Bellefaire/JCB Transitional Living Program. We wish to stress the preliminary nature of this outcome report. Our focus in this paper has been on describing the Bellefaire/JCB Transitional Living Program in as much detail as possible. The professional literature is strong on outcome studies, but weak on descriptions of programs to such an extent that if a professional sought to use the literature to develop his or her own program, it would be difficult to find an adequate description.

METHODS

Subjects

Since the inception of the Bellefaire/JCB Transitional Living Program in 1997, 58 young people (28 males, 30 females) have been served. Two left the program within a few days. Nine are presently enrolled in the program. Forty-nine have completed the program. The majority of those adolescents were referred from public agencies such as the Department of Child and Family Services and the juvenile courts. As such, the majority of those adolescents have had their placements funded by Medicaid or by the court system.

The adolescents in this program have significant, often disabling, psychological and psychiatric disorders. These disorders have often been complicated by long periods of institutional care or by foster care placements that have stressed conformity rather than individual self-respect and initiative. A majority of the adolescents have DSM-IV Axis I diagnoses of Oppositional Defiant Disorder, Conduct Disorder, Post-traumatic Stress Disorder, or Dysthymia, either singly or in combination. Many of the adolescents have I.Q. levels in the borderline mentally-retarded range. Many of the adolescents have been physically or sexually abused.

Procedures

In preparation for this paper, one of the authors (SD) prepared a list of the 47 discharged young people and asked three professionals who had known them for most or all of their stay to categorize them as: (1) More symptomatic at discharge than at admission, i.e., showing new symptoms or new behaviors hurtful to themselves or others, (2) Unchanged by their stay in the program, (3) Improved, that is, showing easily discernable differences in their capacity for comfortable and effective engagement with the non-residential communities of work, school, and family, or (4) Much improved, i.e., striking and continuing changes for 6 months or more in duration in their capacity for comfortable and effective engagement with the non-residential communities of work, school, and family. In a few instances, only two of the three professionals had known the child throughout their stay; in those instances, two reports were examined. The reliability of this gross estimate was approximately 100%, with only a few occurrences with a difference of one category between the assessors.

RESULTS

Change in Symptomatology

The results of the preliminary outcome study suggest that of the 47 adolescents who have completed the program 6% (3 of 47) were considered more symptomatic at discharge than at admission, 30% (14 of 47) were considered not to have shown any change in symptomatology from admission to discharge, 40% (19 of 47) were considered to have shown improvement, and 24% (11 of 47) were considered to have shown significant improvement.

Length of Stay

The results of our preliminary analysis of how length of stay affects outcome indicates that of the 47 adolescents who completed the program, 16 were discharged under six months after their admission, 12 were discharged between six and nine months after their admission, 15 were discharged between nine months to one year after their admission, and 4 were enrolled in the program for more than one year. Of the 16 discharged prior to six months, 2 had more significant symptomatology, 8 showed no significant change, and 6 were improved. Of the 12 discharged between six and nine months, 1 had more significant symptomatology, 2 showed no significant change, 5 were improved, and 4 were much improved. Of the 15 discharged between nine months and one year, none had worsened, 3 showed no significant change, 7 were improved, and 5 were much improved. Of the 4 discharged over one year after their admission, none had worsened, 1 showed no significant change, 1 was improved, and 2 were much improved.

DISCUSSION

In the paper above, we have attempted to describe in considerable detail the structure and content of the Bellefaire/JCB Transitional Living Program. We have used brief case studies in an attempt to add a sense of the clients in our program, how they respond to us, and how we respond to them. We have found it difficult to describe a program that we are in the process of implementing and that is constantly changing. We are hopeful that our readers will find this description helpful.

We are also hopeful about our program as a result of the findings of our preliminary study of client outcome. Those findings include that the change in symptomatology for approximately 64% of our clients was rated as either improved or much improved at discharge as compared to admission. Those findings suggest that an adequate length of stay in the program increases an client's chances of success. For example, results show that while only 38% of clients who were enrolled for under six months were rated as improved or much improved, 77% of clients who were enrolled for over six months were rated as improved or much improved. However, it may simply be that those clients who stay in treatment are less severely disturbed and that this finding is more indicative of severity of disturbance at admission than of an effect of length of stay in the program.

The authors would like to recognize that the above results must be taken as preliminary. Our methods of assessment are crude and were not built into the program from the beginning. They are subjective and have been done by individuals who have a stake in the program. Further, they reflect adjustment at the point of discharge when independent functioning apart from the program had not yet been required of our clients. The advantage of these assessments is that they are based on intimate and professional knowledge of the child as viewed from the milieu. Furthermore, they reflect total functional adaptation to the community at the time of discharge. We attempted to make up for these shortcomings by using measures that are gross and which include assessments easily made and agreed upon by the assessors in almost all instances.

Case Study 4: A One-Year Long Treatment

Samantha had been a resident in another cottage at Bellefaire/JCB prior to her admission to the Transitional Living Program. That cottage was an all-female cottage and Samantha had developed a strong relationship with her prime worker in that cottage. Samantha was described as a leader, although not always in a positive manner. She was transferred to the Transitional Living Program to help her acquire the skills necessary for living independently after her discharge from our programs. Her original admission to Bellefaire/JCB followed a stay at a local juvenile detention home for delinquent young people. She had been charged with domestic violence against her maternal grandmother, who had assumed responsibility for Samantha following her mother's death due to drug overdose. Her diagnoses were Oppositional Defiant Disorder and Borderline Retardation.

Samantha's transition to the Transitional Living Program cottage was a difficult one. After an initial period of positive feelings about the move, she began to complain bitterly about what she perceived as a "lack of attention." She resisted finding her way in the broader community, in seeking employment, and in using public transportation. When confronted with these tasks, she would become tearful, lament the loss of her relationship with the prime worker from her old cottage, and express reservations about the Transitional Living Program expectations. It may be that

Samantha had become upset and overwhelmed by the fact that she was now required to do for herself what the adults in her life had always done for her.

With support, Samantha began to thrive. Her first great triumph was that of securing a job at the concession stand of the local movie theatre. She was simply thrilled to be making money and succeeding "on her own." Eventually, she began to feel that her concession stand job was not fulfilling enough for her, and at a staffing that included her probation officer and grandmother, it became clear that the time had come to begin discussing Samantha's transition back into the community. Although she was still attending the Bellefaire school, she was subsequently discharged to her grandmother's home.

We have tried to emphasize the fundamental place of relationships with adult staff and peers, as well as the provision of a safe, caring, and responsive therapeutic cottage setting that employs a psycho-educational model for the teaching of specific transitional living skills. The result has been a therapeutic community that is in touch with the broader school, community, and family settings. It acknowledges its impermanence and keeps discharge and life after treatment as constant beacons on the horizon.

We believe that we are just beginning to tap the possibilities of working with youth "in transition." These are young people who were destined to experience bleak futures; all are in late adolescence and are in fierce conflict with society, with their families, and with themselves. Few have ever had rewarding significant relationships. Many have spent much of their lives in foster care or in institutions. All are confronting and failing the developmental issue of establishing themselves as young adults with an awareness of the future and a vision of their place in that future.

The program we have described emphasizes responsibility, respect, and relationships. The "Three R's" apply both to residents and staff and although roles may be quite different, the "Three R's" are applicable to everyone connected with the program. In this paper, we have focused on the milieu program in our Transitional Living Cottage, itself a part of an integrated program that includes school, work, psychotherapy, family, and milieu. The preliminary results that we presented in this paper, while impressive, still indicate that 36% of the young people we serve are not noticeably better off when they leave than they were when they were admitted to our program. We see many ways in which we can improve the Transitional Living Program and it is our hope that those changes will help all of the young people we serve free themselves from humiliation, injury, shame, and hurt, as well as from a narrow vision of their own potential to lead better lives.

REFERENCES

Curry, J.F. (1991). Outcome research on residential treatment: Implications and suggested directions. *The American Journal of Orthopsychiatry*, 61(3), 348-357.

Durkin, R.P., and Durkin, A.B. (1975). Evaluating residential treatment programs for disturbed children. In M. Guttentag & E.L. Struenning (Eds.), *Handbook of Evaluation Research* (Vol. 2, 275-339). Newbury Park, CA: Sage Publications.

Leichtman, M., Leichtman, M.L., Barber, C.C., and Neese, D.T. (2001). Effectiveness of intense short-term residential treatment with severely disturbed adolescents. *The American Journal of Orthopsychiatry*, 71(2), 227-235.

BIOGRAPHICAL NOTES

Scott Dowling, MD, is a child, adolescent, and adult psychiatrist and psychoanalyst. He serves as the psychiatrist for the Bellefaire/JCB Transitional Living Program (Shaker Heights, Ohio).

Suellen Saunders, MSSA, LISW, is a licensed social worker with the Bellefaire/JCB Transitional Living Program (Shaker Heights, Ohio).

Cathy Marcus, LSW, is a licensed social worker, who is currently a supervisor at Bellefaire/JCB in the Transitional Living Program (Shaker Heights, Ohio).

Evan Langholt, MSSA, LISW, is a licensed social worker, who is currently a unit supervisor at Bellefaire/JCB in the Transitional Living Program (Shaker Heights, Ohio).

J. Ashby, MSSA, LISW, is a licensed social worker with the Bellefaire/JCB Transitional Living Program (Shaker Heights, Ohio).

Correspondence may be sent to Scott Dowling, MD, Bellefaire/JCB, 22300 South Woodland, Shaker Heights, OH 44122.

Research and Practice
in Social- and Life-Skills Training

D. Patrick Zimmerman, Psyd

SUMMARY. A concern about the development of social and living skills for young people was a part of the very beginnings of residential treatment in the early 1900s and it continued as an important focus in the elaboration of psychodynamic ego psychology in the 1930s. Subsequent to the later emergence and popularity of behavioral and cognitive-behavioral theories and treatment techniques, during the 1980s great interest developed in creating social- and life-skills intervention-training programs for young people displaying impaired interpersonal abilities. This article describes life-skills assessment and training, program effectiveness, and selected model programs. It then reviews some of the currently accepted social-skill assessment techniques and then briefly describes a selected number of commercially published social-skills training programs.

Despite the wide range of currently available programs, contemporary research seems to demonstrate that there remain problems in the area of life-skill outcomes, as well as persisting difficulties with the maintenance and generalization of the social skills achieved by the application of didactic training programs. This article suggests that to the extent that both life-skills and social/interpersonal skills may be embedded in or part of broader, more underlying issues of personality functioning, the attempt to teach them as discrete behavioral tasks which can be dichotomized from those deeper issues may be what contributes to some extent to the difficulties of maintenance and generalization of social-skills training. *[Article copies available for a fee from The Haworth Document Delivery Service: 1-800-*

[Haworth co-indexing entry note]: "Research and Practice in Social- and Life-Skills Training." Zimmerman, D. Patrick. Co-published simultaneously in *Residential Treatment for Children & Youth* (The Haworth Press, Inc.) Vol. 20, No. 2, 2002, pp. 51-75; and: *On Transitions from Group Care: Homeward Bound* (ed: Richard A. Epstein, Jr., and D. Patrick Zimmerman) The Haworth Press, Inc., 2002, pp. 51-75. Single or multiple copies of this article are available for a fee from The Haworth Document Delivery Service [1-800-HAWORTH, 9:00 a.m. - 5:00 p.m. (EST). E-mail address: getinfo@haworthpressinc.com].

51

*HAWORTH. E-mail address: <getinfo@haworthpressinc.com> Website: <http://
www.haworthPress.com> © 2002 by The Haworth Press, Inc. All rights reserved.]*

KEYWORDS. Social skills, life skills, training programs

INTRODUCTION

In his recent brief paper on the issue of "reinventing residential
childcare" in the United States, James Whittaker (2000) noted that residential care continues to be viewed more as part of the problem in services to young people, rather than as part of the solution. Among the
variety of reasons that he cites, some of the difficulties include: the lack
of clear diagnostic indicators for residential placement; a presumption
of "intrusiveness" and concerns about attachment for children placed;
questionable effectiveness of residential treatment; a lack of consensus
on the more important intervention components; a lack of residential
treatment theory development in recent years; and a continuing familial
bias in service selection. Later in his paper, Whittaker cites a number of
characteristics that a recent report of the U. S. Government Accounting
Office (1994) identified as appearing to be related to treatment success
in group care. While two crucial ingredients were family involvement
and the development of adequate post-care community supports, the
findings also included the importance of teaching social, coping, and
living skills as a part of the overall residential treatment experience.
This paper will focus upon the issue of living skills, and especially upon
social-skills training, which may be argued to serve as the building
blocks for successfully teaching life skills that enable young people to
successfully take advantage of transitional and post-program living options.

EARLY HISTORICAL PERSPECTIVES

Although much of the contemporary writings about the implementation of social skills training is based upon behavioral and cognitive-behavioral theories about treatment, it might be argued that one can actually
find references to concerns about such issues in the writings of some of

the early founders of residential treatment for young people. There have been many threads in the historical development of the concept of group care in the United States, but one of the clearest and most direct lines of theory contribution leads back to August Aichhorn's organization of an institution for delinquent boys in Oberhollabrunn, Austria, in 1917 (Zimmerman & Cohler, 1998). His book, *Wayward Youth* (1925/1965), reported on a touching experiment in mental health work with adolescents, his attempts to develop and provide psychological treatment for delinquent young people as an alternative to the punitive atmosphere of threats, punishment, flogging and segregation typical of the existing reformatories of that time. Out of the shambles of a former refugee camp, Aichhorn immersed himself in creating a more benign treatment environment for incorrigible young people, adapting Freud's theories and techniques to his own rehabilitative efforts aimed at understanding and influencing the personality structures of delinquents.

Aichhorn's therapeutic work with delinquents included: (1) the application of Freudian psychoanalytic classical drive theory to reconstructively understand delinquent symptoms; (2) a belief in the critical influence of early personal attachment difficulties (especially regarding the mother) in the later development of delinquent symptoms; (3) the prescription of specific therapeutic techniques, especially emphasizing the promotion and use of the positive transference, within a total, planned environment; and (4) a belief in the significance of the peer group as a means of facilitating individual psychological development. In addition to those more widely known aspects of his treatment philosophy, one can find early references to the potentially beneficial effects of attention to the development of personally fulfilling social and life skills for the charges under his care. For example, in *Wayward Youth* (1925/1965), Aichhorn provided anecdotal case descriptions of how even limited vocational experiences within his residential setting provided important and lasting opportunities for the sublimation of issues such as anti-social grandiosity and personal identity confusion displayed by two young men under his care.

In 1940, as the first Nazi bombing of London was initiated, Anna Freud became concerned for both the physical safety and psychological security of young children exposed to this senseless violence. She mobilized efforts to develop a temporary shelter for these children, which was soon replaced by a more ambitious scheme involving more comprehensive residence programs (Cohler & Zimmerman, 1997). The philosophy underlying the work of the war nurseries was founded largely on the earlier work of Aichhorn. Prior to her monthly reports on work in the war nurseries, Miss Freud's seminal earlier work (1936/1966) had focused upon the ego and its mechanisms of defense. That contribution portrayed the structure of the ego as a psychological apparatus "at war" with the id; it was seen as a center of continual conflict between the drives and the demands of reality and the conscience.

Her friend Heinz Hartmann subsequently shifted the focus from the ego as an agency of conflict to a psychic mechanism of positive adaptation to the social world, and he particularly described a number of "conflict-free" functions of the ego (1939/1958). These "conflict free" functions of the ego included: perception, motivation, object comprehension, thinking, language, memory, productivity, the maturation of motor development, and the learning processes inherent in the acquisition of those skills. Seen otherwise, Hartmann's work represented a shift from Anna Freud's emphasis upon the psychological defenses, to the elaboration of a broad range of adaptive developmental and *social/life* skills. A somewhat later elaboration (White & Gilliland, 1975) of the major functions said to comprise the psychological agency often designated as the ego included: perception, consciousness, memory, attention, thought, intelligence, speech/language, motor skills, judgment/foresight, delay of needs and impulses, defenses, and signal affects/emotions (anxiety, depression, shame and guilt). The main reason for enumerating those functions is, once again, to indicate the similarity and relevance of those "ego" capacities to some of our current ideas about "life and social skills."

Turning to a different thread in the development of early ideas about life and social skills, among the most significant contributions of the social sciences to the study of personal development has been a focus on the meanings that are made of one's environment or of the total "life surround." The social psychologist Kurt Lewin (1943, 1944) referred to this totality of experience as the "life-space," noting that particular behavior is a function of both the person and his/her psychologically relevant environment. All aspects of intention and action are governed by the meanings with which the child endows the psychologically relevant field experienced at a particular time. As Lewin (1943) observed, "Any behavior or any other change in a psychological field depends . . . upon the psychological field at that time" (p. 45). While the past as presently experienced is a critically important determinant of this present experience of the life-space, focus is on the experience of this life-space as the present psychologically meaningful determinant of intention and action.

Much of Lewin's pioneering work led to contemporary social psychology and to the study of collective behavior; his contributions have had different important contributions in the field of psychology. First, as interpreted by Redl and Wineman's writings on group care (1951, 1952), the focus on the personally significant life-space, and the interplay of life space and group process, provided a model for realizing change among troubled young people unable to live with others and experiencing personal disorganization. Redl and Wineman emphasized Lewin's concept of life-space in their effort to intervene in the lives of troubled children, blending the insights gained from Lewin's portrayal of the experience of self and others within group and society with the emerging theories of ego psychology during the post-war period, in the construction of a childrens' center which would foster enhanced ego control among children whose egos were unable to perform as a consequence of early life experiences of poverty and both social and family disorganization.

Their work at Pioneer House in Detroit, Michigan, sought to integrate the classical drive-oriented perspective on work with delinquent children first formulated by Aichhorn (1925), the tradition of psychoanalytic ego psychology and education initiated by Anna Freud and Heinz Hartmann, as well as the social psychology insights realized from the studies by Lewin and his colleagues. Indeed, Redl and Wineman (1951) began their first book with an explicit acknowledgement to Aichhorn, a statement of the direct lineage of their thinking to this signal figure in psychoanalysis, who was among the first to apply a psychoanalytic understanding of motivation to education and the first to attempt to understand delinquency in the same terms as neurotic symptoms. While Redl and Wineman are perhaps best known for their attempts to develop specific strategies for child care workers to deal with the difficulties of working with aggressive, delinquent young people, those strategies can also be understood as attempts to enhance the "ego strengths" of those children or, said otherwise, to develop social awareness and increased social coping and life skills.

CURRENT FINDINGS ON THE STATUS OF LIFE-SKILLS TRAINING

Difficulties Experienced by Young Persons Leaving Alternate Care

Barth (1993) noted that life-skills training has been one of the latest additions to the scenery of school districts across the United States, as part of a greater concern about the human condition of their students. The issue is of even greater importance for youth who are leaving different out-of-home care settings, especially residential treatment. For example, the 1990 Westat study (Cook, 1990) found that only 44 percent of the

18-year-olds discharged from out-of-home care had completed high school at the time of discharge to independence. Further, only 39 percent had any job experience, 38 percent had been clinically diagnosed as emotionally disturbed, 58 percent had three or more different living placements prior to discharge and 29 percent reported drug abuse or alcohol problems. The 1992 National Association of Social Worker survey (Bass, 1992) of runaway and homeless young persons documented the same kind of difficulties by adolescents served in emergency shelters: 53 percent had educational problems, 26 percent had a mental health problem, 20 percent had attempted suicide, 23 percent had abused drugs, 19 percent had abused alcohol and 39 percent had no means of financial support.

Lindsey and Ahmed's (1999) review of follow-up studies of former foster wards presents similar results, concluding that these young people were likely to have serious educational deficits, to be unemployed or employed in low-paying jobs, to have difficulties in securing satisfactory housing, and to be in receipt of some form of public assistance. Despite the alarming numbers noted above, the 1988 Westat study of young persons leaving out-of-home care found that 68 percent had not received services in money management/consumer awareness, 69 percent had received no training in decision making/problem solving skills, 71 percent had received no services in the area of food management, 71 percent had received no assistance in the knowledge of community resources, 76 percent had received no services in post-discharge housing skills, and 82 percent had received no documented training related to emergency/safety skills. Given that this national survey is over ten years old, one might have justifiable concerns about how much this situation has improved since that time.

On the other hand, with the impetus of some increased federal and state funding for transitional services, a number of programs have been developed at the state and local levels, which offer a number of services focussing upon a myriad of life-skills training components. Most of these programs dichotomously divide the training skills into hard, tangible, or resource life skills versus soft, intangible, or functional life skills (Cook & Ansell, 1986; Hahn, 1994; Nollan, Wolf, Ansell, Burns, Barr, Copeland, & Paddock, 2000). The former tend to be defined as skills that the young person must *know or do* to meet specific independent living needs such as employment, housing, money management, resources for leisure and recreation, transportation knowledge and home management. The latter focus more upon the individual's development of self-esteem and other personality attributes such as cognitive problem-solving skills, communication skills, anger management, and social skills.

In terms of the actual delivery of life-skills, Ansell (2001) has presented an instructional model pictured as a four-stage independent living continuum. Phase 1 involves "Informal" exposure to life skills, through mentoring, informal group discussions, helping with group activities and work shadowing. Phase 2, "Formal" activities, includes one-to-one and group life-skills teaching and activities, as well as field trips and service projects. Phase 3 involves "Supervised Independent Living" programs, with supervised apartments and other transitional living arrangements. The final stage, Phase 4, is the stage of "Self-Sufficiency," and involves the use of support groups, counseling, and the active provision of information and referral services. Ansell states that during the past ten years, most of the life-skills work has been done in Phase 2 ("Formal Learning") on the continuum, but that the area in which we can expect the most development in the near future is in Phase 3, "Supervised Independent Living."

Effectiveness of Life-Skills Training

Despite the efforts to increase services to provide life-skills training, questions remain about the effectiveness of these services. In one effort to evaluate the need for life-skills training, Mech, Ludy-Dobson, and Hulseman (1994) surveyed the levels of life-skill knowledge for youth living in different out-of-home settings. Their findings revealed higher life-skills mean score knowledge levels for young people in scattered (158.70) and clustered (150.09) independent living apartment arrangements, followed by young people living in foster homes (148.46) and residential institutions (138.23). Young people living in group home settings appeared to show the lowest levels of life-skill knowledge, with a mean score of 133.50. While Mech et al. (1994) developed their own life-skills assessment inventory, there are a number of other useful assessment tools. Life-skills assessment inventories currently in use include: the Tests of Everyday Living (TEL-McGraw Hill Publishers), the Daniel Memorial Independent Living Skills System, the Life Skills Inventory Summary Report Form, the Independent Living Skills Assessment Tool, the Scales of Independent Behavior and the Vineland Adaptive Behavior Scales. An especially useful tool is the Ansell-Casey Life Skills Assessment, which has excellent psychometric properties and is now available at no cost on the Internet.

In terms of programs offering life-skill and transitional-living training, a relatively recent Westat national report (Cook, 1994) examined the effect of independent living skills training on eight outcomes and found no significant difference between young people that received no training and young persons that had received some skills training. However, in a subset of the research, the study did find that training in multiple skill areas, specifically training in the five core areas of budgeting, obtaining credit, consumer credit, education, and employment was associated with better outcomes.

With the passage of P. L. 99-272, and more recently P. L. 106-109, federal support has enabled states to develop Individual Living Programs for young persons in need of life-skills services, and there has been some beginning research on those state-wide programs. For example, regarding the Nebraska life-skills training initiative, the Center on Children, Families and the Law (1994) conducted a survey which found that youth who received some type of life-skills training help were no more likely than those who reported receiving no help to feel more prepared to live independently. Shippensburg University (1993) evaluated Pennsylvania's Independent Living Program (ILP) and found that only two of the seven outcome measures indicated any significant differences between ILP participants and nonparticipants. On the other hand, Lindsey and Ahmed (1999) evaluated North Carolina's Independent Living Program (ILP) and found modest, although mixed, gains for participants when compared to nonparticipants. Mech (1999) has indicated that given the problematic outcomes cited in the evaluation research there is a critical need for a unified research strategy, especially so because life-skills training and independent living programs are now national in scope. Among his suggestions are the development of a more unified data collection base, as well as a research model with a core set of performance measures or outcome indicators.

Life-Skills/Independent Living Model Programs

Despite the equivocal outcome results of life-skills/transitional programs, a number of particular programs have been cited as models of useful training. While it is certainly beyond the range of this paper to provide a comprehensive overview of the many model programs in existence now, a select number have been described in the literature as promising efforts in this area. Some of these programs have included: Preparation of Youth for Employment (PYE) developed by the Casey Family Programs' Walnut Creek (California) Division, the Tucson Self-Sufficiency Program (Arizona), the Job Development Initiative (JDI) in Austin, Texas and the Thresholds Transitional Living Program in Chicago (IL). The

Boysville of Michigan Supervised Independent Living Program (SIL) has published a one year follow-up of its life-skills program (Hoge & Idalski, 2001), but with somewhat mixed results. Former residents made noticeable gains in full- or part-time employment, but there was also a decline in the percentage of former residents still living a legal lifestyle. The Work Appreciation for Youth Program (WAY), developed at Children's Village (Dobbs Ferry, New York), has published a 15-year longitudinal study of the program demonstrating many positive long-term effects.

CONTEMPORARY VIEWS OF SOCIAL-SKILLS TRAINING

The relationship between life-skills training and social skills training is a bit like the statistical worth of educational, vocational or psychological tests. For example, we know that if a test is unreliable, it cannot have statistical validity. Metaphorically, this may also be true for the relationship between life-skills training and social-skills training. As Cook (1994) has pointed out, even though we often refer to social skills as part of the soft or intangible part of life-skills training, in fact it appears to have a much more important role than suggested by those terms. Cook observed that social skills may not be found to be statistically related to life-skills outcomes, but that does not mean that they are not effective in producing better outcomes. In essence, social skills seem to form the bedrock of life-skill achievements, an integral part of the performance of life-skills that is difficult to segregate in outcome analysis of life-skills achievement and performance.

In terms of the development of social-skills training, which may form the foundation for life-skills performance, it is useful once again to turn attention to the historical background of what has developed today into social-skills training programs. Kurt Lewin's contributions have been mentioned earlier in this paper, and his very earliest writings about social field theory had a second major impact which has been important for the development of current ideas about both social-skills and life-skills training. Lewin's emphasis upon the importance of construing human behavior as the joint function of the individual and his particular environmental circumstances was influential in setting the stage for the emergence of the behavior therapist's view of personality as referring basically to the individual's conditioned responses as learned abilities or skills to cope with various life events. The later introduction of more cognitive factors into the behavior therapist's understanding of personality change was associated with the emergence and development of cognitive-behavioral therapy, one of today's most widely endorsed forms of psychotherapy. While it is beyond the scope of this paper to elaborate upon the many types of clinical interventions characteristic of behavioral techniques and of cognitive-behavioral therapy, it must be emphasized that both forms of treatment are crucial to the popularity of present-day conceptions of social- and life-skills training, since the latter models of service delivery are almost always based upon behavioral or cognitive-behavioral theories. For example, most social-skills training packages use a blend of behavioral and cognitive-behavioral techniques that could include modeling, rehearsal and role-playing, performance feedback, removal of problem behaviors through reinforcement and/or reductive procedures, self-instruction and self-evaluation (including the modification of distorted thinking and belief systems), as well as training for generalization and maintenance of skills (including social skills homework assignments).

Other important influences which contributed to the burgeoning popularity of social-skills training programs have included the renewed interest since the 1960s in certain theories of child and adolescent development, specifically including Piaget's theories of cognitive development, Erikson's theory of psychosocial development, Kohlberg's theory of moral development, and Goleman's theories about emotional intelligence.

Assessment Techniques for Social-Skills Training

As with the application of any behavioral or cognitive-behavioral treatment program, social-skills training begins with the assessment procedure and emphasizes direct and objective measurement approaches (as distinguished from projective personality techniques). These techniques include the direct observation of social skills, as well as the use of behavioral rating scales, sociometric techniques and objective self-report methods.

Direct Observation. Direct observation techniques are based in behavioral theory and applied behavioral analysis; they are said to have a high degree of treatment validity. Observational coding procedures can generally be broken down into four types of coding or recording methods: event recording, interval recording, time-sample recording and duration/latency recording.

Behavior Rating Scales. Behavior rating scales utilize ratings by informants who know the child well, often a teacher, parent, or professional caretaker. A sample of six widely used rating scales in the field of social-skills assessment and training includes: the Behavioral Assessment System of Children (BASC), the Matson Evaluation of Social Skills with Youngsters (MESSY), the Preschool and Kindergarten Behavior Scales (PKBS), the School Social Behavior Scales (SSBS), the Social Skills Rating System (SSRS) and the Walker-McConnell Scales of Social Competence and School Adjustment (SSCSA).

Sociometric Techniques. Sociometric techniques obtain information from within a peer group (usually classmates) and measure qualities such as popularity, acceptance or rejection status, leadership ability, athletic or academic skills, aggressiveness, and social comfort or discomfort. Four examples of sociometric techniques are: peer nomination, picture sociometrics, "guess who" measures, and the classroom play.

Objective Self-Report Tests. Examples of these include the Assessment of Interpersonal Relations (AIR) and the Social Skills Rating System (SSRS).

Some advocate that when possible, the best social skills assessment practice involves the use of an aggregated multiple assessment model, utilizing subject interviews, direct observation, behavior rating scales, sociometric and self-report measures.

A Selective Review of Social-Skills Training Programs

Although with the great increase in the use of social-skills training programs one might expect to find a commonly accepted taxonomy of social skills, this is not yet the case. Nevertheless, one good general framework of basic social skills categories was developed by Stephens (1978) and described in greater detail by Cartledge and Milburn (1986). According to this framework, social skills can be divided into four general categories: Self-Related Behaviors, Environmental Behaviors, Task-Related Behaviors and Interpersonal Behaviors. The four general categories can be further analyzed into 30 subcategories, and even further into 136 specific social skills under those general categories and subcategories. Another classification system, Caldarella and Merrell (1997) used a multivariate approach to 21 studies of social skills in programs that dealt with over 22,000 children and adolescents. Five primary social-skills dimensions were identified, including: peer relations, self-management, academics, compliance, and assertion. Those dimensions included nearly thirty more specific descriptors, each of which could be subdivided into a substantially larger number of specific social skills. As can be concluded from the two examples of categorization given above, the wide variety of social skills which might be targeted in a particular training program can make the development of a unique program a truly formidable task, and argues favorably for the use of programs which have already been developed and commercially published for wider use. A description of six major commercially published social-skills training programs follows, a description that is only presented as a brief sampling of the wider range of programs available today.

1. *The Skillstreaming Series.* The Skillstreaming approach is geared to three specific age levels: preschool/kindergarten, elementary, and adolescence. The preschool level (McGinnis & Goldstein, 1990) involves 40 beginning-level prosocial skills. The elementary level (McGinnis, Goldstein, Sprafkin, & Gershaw, 1984), 60 prosocial skills, aims at classroom survival skills, friendship-making, dealing with feelings, alternatives to aggression, and skills for dealing with stress. The adolescent level (Goldstein, Sprafkin, Gershaw, & Klein, 1980), with 50 skills, focuses on beginning and advanced social skills, dealing with feelings, alternatives to aggression, dealing with stress, and planning skills. The Skillstreaming programs are designed for use in both the classroom and in more clinical settings. *The Aggression Replacement Program* (ART) is closely related to the Skillstreaming programs and is aimed for use with juvenile delinquents or other adolescents (Goldstein, Blick, Reiner, Zimmerman, & Coultry, 1987). It teaches 10 prosocial skills, anger-control, and moral education. *The Prepare Curriculum* (Goldstein, 1988) is another Skillstreaming-related program for use with elementary and high school-age young people. It consists of 10 courses, many of which are similar to the Skillstreaming and ART program components.

2. *(Classic): The Culture and Lifestyle Appropriate Social Skills Intervention Curriculum* (Dygon, 1993). The CLASSIC is a behaviorally oriented social-skills curriculum of 15 lessons for small-group instruction of children and adolescents with at least an average level of intelligence. The emphasis is to teach children to be more accepted by their peers, with an emphasis on cross-cultural social appropriateness. There are no set target behaviors; instead, each group identifies behaviors that are socially acceptable in their particular social setting. Behavior identification is achieved by group members generating lists of behaviors exhibited by children they like and do not like, and these lists are used as referent points during the program sessions.

3. *The Metacognitive Approach to Social Skills Training (MASST).* The MASST program (Sheinker & Sheinker, 1988) is used with young people in grades 4 through 12, and is intended to teach them how to be self-directive, to self-monitor, to self-evaluate, and to self-correct. The 40-unit package is divided into five parts: (1) Who am I? Self-concept;

(2) Where am I going: Goal setting; (3) How will I become the person I choose to be? (4) How do I get what I want from others and from myself? and (5) Who is in charge?

4. *The Assist Program: Affective-Social Skills: Instructional Strategies and Techniques (ASSIST).* The ASSIST program (Huggins, 1990-1995) is intended for use with elementary school students and focuses primarily on teaching friendship skills, self-esteem, anger management, and cooperation skills.

5. *The Social Skills Intervention Guide: Practical Strategies for Social Skills Training* (Elliott & Gresham, 1991). This social skills intervention package was designed to be used with the Social Skills Rating System, an assessment tool described earlier in this paper. The program is a behavioral program that covers 43 social skills in five areas measured by the SSRS: cooperation, assertion, responsibility, empathy and self-control.

6. *Teaching Social Skills to Youth: A Curriculum for Child-Care Providers* (Dowd & Tierney, 1992). This program was developed at Boys Town (Nebraska), and the social skill deficits targeted for training are inferred from DSM-IV diagnostic classifications. The manual covers 182 social skills, divided into basic, intermediate, advanced, and complex levels. The range of skills extends from accepting "no" for an answer and "introducing yourself" (basic) to conflict resolution, goal setting and seeking professional assistance (complex). Users of the program must be familiar with the teaching techniques developed at Boystown and presented in the first part of the program manual.

EFFECTIVENESS OF SOCIAL-SKILLS TRAINING PROGRAMS

Training with Differing Diagnostic Groups

Evaluation research focusing upon the effectiveness of social-skills training with young persons displaying differing types of emotional or behavioral problems has provided mixed results. Merrell and Gimpel (1998) have reviewed the literature on the use of such training with young persons with either internalizing (depression and social withdrawal) or externalizing (anti-social/aggressive and ADHD) problems. In terms of internalizing problems, it appears that social-skills training is best utilized as part of a broad intervention package. Thus, the research has often been unclear about to what extent the social skills component contributes to the improvement in comparison to the other treatment components. For example, in terms of depression, little is really known about the effectiveness of social skills training compared to the other modes of treatment used as components of the broader intervention approach for child and adolescent depression. Studies have supported the use of social-skills training with socially isolated or withdrawn young persons, although here again the results have been somewhat varied.

With regard to young people with more externalizing problems, there appears to be a positive but limited effect on the sometimes impaired social behaviors of children and adolescents with ADHD. However, because the research with this group has been noticeably limited, no strong conclusions can be drawn at this time about the efficacy of social-skills training with young persons exhibiting ADHD symptoms. In terms of social-skills training for antisocial-aggressive children, there have been some particular outcome reports of positive effects. For example, Reddy and Goldstein (2001) discuss a limited number of studies that lend some support for the effectiveness of the Aggression Replacement Training program with juvenile delinquents. Lochman, Curry, Dane, and Ellis (2001) reported effectiveness for the Anger Coping Program for aggressive or impulsive boys, although "booster sessions" were required for longer-term maintenance of skills. In general, however, the effects often have been modest in terms of practical significance (Merrell & Gimpel, 1998). In other words, severely antisocial-aggressive children and adolescents appear to be quite resistant to even the best-planned and implemented social-skills interventions. Moreover, as is many times the case with other treatment groups, the maintenance of changes over time is frequently an issue. When gains are achieved, it is not uncommon for those achievements to disappear within several months.

Children and adolescents with learning disabilities may also display poor peer relationships, a seeming lack of social-skills competence and behaviors that over time can come to bear a resemblance to the conduct disorders. Some years ago, Trapani (1990) noted that although social skills-training has been used with persons with learning disabilities, it has not consistently proven to be a valid procedure for the treatment of social skills-deficits with this group. Trapani observed that when research has been able to document an improvement in the quality and frequency of social interaction in the treatment setting, these changes often do not transfer to the natural setting.

Maintenance and Generalization of Social Skills

This problem with the generalization of skill gains has been described in the evaluation research as a difficulty applying to social-skills training overall. Quite recently, Grizenko, Zappitelli, Langevin, Hrycho, El-Messidi, Kaminester, Pawliuk, and Stepanian (2000) reviewed numerous studies of the effectiveness of social-skills training and identified several problems in the evaluation research. These difficulties included the questionable effectiveness of socially valid measures, including the use of sociometric measures such as peer nomination and peer exclusion, measures that have been shown to have low stability estimate scores. A major obstacle, however, has been the previously noted failure of generalization of acquired skills both across time and between ecologically relevant settings.

For example, Schneider (1992) used a meta-analysis of 79 social-skills training studies published between 1942 and 1987 and found that, overall, short-term effectiveness was only moderate, with only nine studies using follow-up intervals longer than three months. Beelmann, Pfingsten, and Losel (1994) applied meta-analysis procedures to the effects of 49 studies published from 1981 to 1990 and found that social-skills training was moderately effective in the short term, but that there were no significant follow-up and long-term effects. Grizenko et al. (2000) concluded that although many single studies have demonstrated moderate short-term positive effects for social-skills training, there is still no strong evidence that supports a conclusion that such programs have had significant long-term effects. In addition, they observed, the task of overall evaluation of social-skills training is an arduous and elusive one because of the vast number of studies that have been reported and the wide variations in investigator designs, methodologies, and outcome assessments. Further, they note, even when a combination of several training modalities (modeling, reinforcement techniques, cognitive problem-solving, self-control training) has been utilized, the problem of poor generalization remains.

In an attempt to remedy this disappointing limitation to social-skills training (Merrell & Gimpel, 1998) have proposed that careful planning and attention to what is referred to as *transfer training* needs to be an important component of social-skills programs from the very outset of this type of treatment intervention. As one example of the techniques which might prove to enhance the generalization of skills, Cartledge and Milburn (1995) suggested five possible approaches: (1) training in different settings, (2) training with a variety of staff members, (3) developing cognitive expectancies of success, (4) changing the timing, nature and source of reinforcements, and (5) developing self-management skills (self-monitoring, self-evaluation, self-reinforcement). In summary, according to the perspective presented by Cartledge and Milburn, the child or adolescent must learn to manage their thinking and behaviors so that a dependency upon external factors for generalization is reduced. The present author would add that the child or adolescent must *want* to learn to manage their thinking and behaviors, which is an entirely different clinical endeavor.

While arguments against behavioral and cognitive-behavioral techniques have been commonplace from psychodynamic perspectives, it is interesting to note that there have been some recent criticisms from within the behavioral field itself. As one example, John Staddon (2001) proposes a new theoretical model of behaviorism, which presents detailed criticisms of the Skinnerian foundation of behaviorism, and of the more recent evolution of cognitive psychology. While it is beyond the scope of this paper to present Staddon's experimentally based arguments in detail, it is important to note a number of his disagreements with classical behaviorism as an instrumental or operant conditioning model. Among Staddon's observations, which differ dramatically from staunchly traditional behaviorists, are that: (1) only *some things* that animals (and by inference humans) do can be selected through operant reinforcement; (2) real-life social questions cannot always be the subject of meaningful experiments, and . . . our ignorance of fundamentals severely limits our ability to generalize from laboratory situations to the world at large; (3) knowing the causal chain or predictability of events does not necessarily deny the existence of human free agency or the genuine feeling of freedom; behaviorism cannot continue to define the realm of values as just reinforcers derived via the mechanism of conditioned reinforcement if it is to have any practical or social worth to man; and (4) human behaviors, preferences, and learning are not solely dependent upon past experiences, or as Skinner would put it, past histories of reinforcements. In terms of cognition, Staddon readmits the importance of internal private events, as well as the world of both conscious and unconscious realms of cognition.

Staddon is somewhat equivocal about the advances of cognitive psychology. For example, cognitive-behavioral psychotherapy depends heavily upon the concept of cognitive "schemas," which in turn depend upon an assumption that internal mental representations truly exist. On the one hand, Staddon admits that a few ingenious studies provide results which are consistent with the idea that some perception involves a "mental representation" with properties quite similar to the real object. Unfortunately, according to Staddon, modern cognitive psychology assumes that those few studies are perfectly general, that the "copy theory" of perception is universally valid. On the other hand, Staddon cites other studies from the field of artificial intelligence which argue that there is no special internal cognitive representation of the external world. Or, those studies propose, such representations are unreliable by-products of the unintelligent action of more or less independent, simple cognitive processes. In other words, the world of schemas and cognitive distortions common to cognitive-behavioral therapy may not be as scientifically demonstrable as we have been persuaded in part by the excitement of developments in that field. In light of his review of wide-ranging empirical evidence, Stoddard advises that regarding both behaviorism and cognitive psychology we would do well to lower our sights and return to a study of the dynamics of simple animal behavior. Direct extrapolation to humans, according to Staddon, is a bit like reaching for the stars instead of reaching for the more useful telescope. In the meantime, we should continue to value the subjective, phenomenological domain of our lives, even *if* positivistic science has nothing to say about it. "[Surely], phenomenal experience is worth something. . . . After all, percepts seem to be so rich, so detailed, so real. About the vividness, we can say (scientifically) nothing. But about the richness of detail, we can say at least this: If the brain is a classifier, it is a very capacious one" (p. 176).

THE LEGACY OF TRADITIONAL BEHAVIORAL AND COGNITIVE-BEHAVIORAL THERAPIES

As proposed in the early part of this paper, it is plausible to consider that concerns about social skill and interpersonal effectiveness can be traced to August Aichhorn's early writings about group care, and soon thereafter similar concerns were apparent in Heinz Hartmann's writings about the "conflict-free" and adaptive ego functions. The work of Kurt Lewin and his focus on the importance of interactive influences with the environment or "life surround" was useful in Fritz Redl's conceptualizations of residential treatment; it also, somewhat paradoxically, helped to foster more behavioral treatment approaches, emphasizing theories of social learning through environmental consequences and reinforcements.

Unfortunately, the early forms of radical behaviorism did much to eliminate intra-psychic issues and matters related to "the mind" from psychology. In other words, the subjective world of man came to be off limits for empirical psychology, since it was not directly observable. In more recent years, that trend has been somewhat reversed, and the mind has been readmitted as a subject of legitimate inquiry for psychology with the advent and popularity of cognitive-behavioral theories and techniques.

However, the version of "the mind" that was initially re-admitted to psychology by the cognitive-behaviorists was an objectivist model, the mind as something akin to the computer with specific rules, formal systems, and cognitive representational schemas. This more or less "scientific" model of the mind was a basically a pragmatic one, marginalizing the realm of human unconscious meaning. Proposing that any *real* human problem could be posed and solved solely through the application of practical reason, this new version of the human mind in psychology lacked a sense of real depth, an interest in the myriad layers of meaning that might be obscure to our own immediate understanding, in favor of a view of ourselves that was more or less completely transparent and immediately knowable to ourselves (Lear, 1998).

The shifts from psychodynamic to behavioral and then cognitive-behavioral techniques were later associated with the proliferation of social- and life-skills training programs as didactic enterprises. Nevertheless, despite the hopefulness about such programs, we are currently left with two quite major dilemmas: (1) only moderate and short-term levels of effectiveness and (2) a frequent lack of treatment generalization. The proposed remedies tend to remain on an external, social learning level–either provide "booster sessions" to improve maintenance of treatment gains, or train across settings to promote generalization. On the other hand, it may well be that either behavioral or classical cognitive-behavioral techniques presented in didactic, manualized training programs may not suffice for the real development of firm social- and life-skill achievements.

TRANSITIONS IN COGNITIVE THERAPY THEORY AND TECHNIQUES

In the more common forms of traditional cognitive-behavioral therapy (CBT), the rational is strengthened to get "on top" of the disturbance. This, of course, might be seen by some as facilitating a split between the rational versus the irrational, as well as between the conscious and the unconscious. The CBT therapist, then, assumes a tutorial relationship with the patient, who is seen as a good and reasonable "victim" of his/her misunderstandings and who is usually assumed to be willing to learn from new cognitive experiences. The psychodynamic therapist, on the other hand, assumes that we learn also from emotional experiences, and that we play an active part in what we learn or mislearn. Unlike the cognitive-behavioral patient, who is generally assumed to be willing to learn about his/her cognitive distortions, the psychodynamic patient is acknowledged to be often quite unwilling to face symptoms, often cannot tolerate knowing or acknowledging the symptoms as such or what rests beneath them.

Interestingly, however, just as in the past there was a drift from behavioral to cognitive-behavioral thinking, in recent years we have witnessed some drift from cognitive-behavioral toward certain aspects of psychoanalytic, or at least psychodynamic, thinking. For instance, as CBT has begun to work with patients suffering from personality disorders (rather than just depression or anxiety), CBT and Cognitive Analytic Therapy (CAT) theory and techniques have begun to be influenced more by ideas about transference phenomena, the unconscious (although defined as generally limited to a cognitive unconscious, rather including affective components), the emotions (understood in terms of serial, rather than parallel architecture) and more attention to the nature of the treatment relationship. CBT has evolved into something less mechanistic, previously reflected in a tendency for the therapist to impose their own "rationality" on the patient, becoming more interested in constructivist theories about how the patient creates his/her reality, object relations, attachment theory, and interpersonal (in addition to cognitive) deficits (Milton, 2001). Even Beck (Beck, A. T., Freeman, A., & Associates, 1990) has proposed longer treatments, increased treatment frequencies, the importance of knowing about the patient's "total life," the value of understanding "here and now" affective experiences within the treatment relationship, and the usefulness of not focusing too much or too prematurely on cognitions and tasks. Nevertheless, there remain substantive differences between the CBT, CAT, and psychodynamic approaches. The former are still distinguished from the psychodynamic approach by their emphasis on cognitive rather than affective learning, reliance upon certain hallmark structural features and assignments, and the CBT and CAT therapist's active assertion of the benign colleague/teacher stance.

CONTINUING CHALLENGES FOR SOCIAL-SKILLS TRAINING

Just as there has been some shift in CBT toward ideas previously associated with psychodynamic thinking, there has been a similar shift in some of the social-skills training curriculums. In addition to the more behavioral aspects of social skills, some programs are moving toward the teaching of skills which sound as though they might have more emotional dimensions, including empathy, moral reasoning and self/other perspective taking. On the other hand, the instructional methodology continues to be based on traditional behavioral and cognitive-behavioral techniques and didactic in approach. There is little that could be described as anything approaching a psychodynamic or affective group-process learning approach in the social-skills training programs available today. To the extent that interpersonal abilities might have an individual, intrapsychic affective component, the absence of a systematic technical attention to this dimension may well play some part in the failure to maintain or generalize initially achieved specific skills. In other words, to the extent that social/interpersonal skills are part of broader, more underlying issues of personality functioning, the attempt to teach them as dichotomized from those deeper issues may be what contributes to some extent, perhaps even largely, to the difficulties of maintenance and generalization of social-skills training.

Another difficulty relates to social-skills training as a didactic approach, based upon a step-wise arrangement of lesson plans. In particular, such a manner of enhancing interpersonal life shares the same difficulties as individual psychotherapy mandated treatment manuals, so popular in our age of managed care in the field of mental health. Such manualized treatments are based upon a number of fictions, including: (1) that there are such things as an average patient with an average case of a particular disorder; (2) that teaching or treatment will inevitably progress from step or stage A, to B, to C in an invariant progression; (3) and that patients will eagerly give up their symptoms or, in our case, social skills deficits. It is probably more true to the matter that people are quite attached to their symptoms and difficulties, and that no amount of teaching of social skills can predict if and when they will give up their difficulties or learn the proposed skills. That depends on when or whether they *decide* to let go of their problem behaviors. Problem behaviors are *not* like viral or bacterial infections that have a natural course when treated with an antibiotic. In the case of interpersonal competencies, social-skills training is talking with real people about real choices about which they might or *might not* be able to make personal decisions and life changes over time. Said otherwise, aside from the training itself, young people are relatively free agents in terms of whether or not they *want* to learn the skills, and later in terms of whether or not they want to perform them.

A final difficulty in conceptualizing social-skills training is illustrated by the attempt of Merrell and Gimpel (1998) to ground social-skills development in various theories of child and adolescent development. Those authors relate the cognitive growth of children and adolescents to Piaget's model of cognitive development. While this could sound authoritative to many readers, there are many crucial difficulties with Piaget's theories, including: (1) his original sample of subjects consisted solely of his own nieces and nephews; (2) the experiments were not characteristic of what children meet in their real world experiences; (3) and his model of invariant stages of cognitive development have been critically challenged by later research in cognitive development.

In terms of psychosocial development, Merrel and Gimpel rely upon Erik Erikson's stages of psychosocial development. This model also has severe limitations, such as: (1) much of the model is *not* an innovation at all, but rather simply a heuristic reframing of the oral, anal, phallic, oedipal, latency, and adolescence stages of Freud's psychosexual model of development; (2) Erikson's stages were not based upon infant, child, or adolescent developmental observations; (3) and, finally, his concept of stages gives the same impression as Piaget's model, i.e., that the stages are invariantly progressive, which later empirical research has clearly disputed.

Next, Merrell and Gimpel rely upon Kohlberg's model of moral development as a basis for the moral dimension of social skills development. Kohlberg's model has glaring deficits: (1) his sample included only Harvard University undergraduates; (2) there were no females in his sample; (3) the moral dilemmas with which his subjects were presented were not reflective of decisions that young people normally need to make in their lives; (4) and his moral stages were based upon a rule-based model, which some have disputed as quite different from the way girls and young women make moral decisions.

Finally, Merrell and Gimpel pay homage to Daniel Goleman's book, *Emotional Intelligence: Why It Can Matter More than IQ*, as an important work that substantiates the need and importance of social-skills training. While the present author concurs with the importance of interpersonal competencies and healthy relationships, Goleman's work is certainly not a major, innovative, or groundbreaking effort in this area. In the first place, it could lead some readers to assume a false dichotomy between cognitive and emotional functioning, realms of functioning that quite probably highly interpenetrate each other. More seriously, however, when one distills the central ingredients of what Goleman presents as his major contribution about emotional intelligence, one finds that the major affective skills that he has summarized are quite commonplace and already well-known, including: self-awareness; identifying, expressing, and managing feelings; impulse control and the delay of gratification; and the ability to handle stress and anxiety. Not only is none of this new or innovative, the constellation of skills that he presents have long been the focus of projective personality assessment, nowhere more clearly and empirically elaborated than in the more current versions of John Exner's comprehensive system of Rorschach interpretation (Exner, 2000). As with other social skills, to what extent these aspects of "emotional intelligence" can be taught to young persons in a didactic manner is still a matter of long-term evaluation research.

CONCLUSION

It can be argued that a concern about the development of social and living skills for young people was a part of the very beginnings of residential treatment in the early 1900s and it continued as an important focus in the elaboration of psychodynamic ego psychology in the 1930s. Subsequent to the later emergence and popularity of behavioral and cognitive-behavioral theories and treatment techniques, during the 1980s great interest developed in creating social- and life-skills intervention-training programs for young people displaying impaired interpersonal abilities. This article reviewed some of the currently accepted life- and social-skill assessment techniques and then briefly described a selected number life-skills model programs and commercially published social-skills training programs.

However, despite the wide range of currently available programs, contemporary research seems to demonstrate that there remain persisting problems in life-skills outcomes, as well as with the maintenance and generalization of the social skills achieved by the application of didactic training programs. Further, with regard to social-skill training it is not yet clear that "booster sessions" or training in differing life settings will resolve those problems with social-skill training interventions. In addition, while there have been some shifts in cognitive-behavioral therapy (upon which many components of social-skills training programs are based) away from the more mechanistic techniques, it is not clear that those shifts alone will significantly affect the current problems in maintenance and generalization. Finally, it has been suggested that many of the models of child and adolescent development, upon which some authors have attempted to ground the development of social-skills training and acquisition, are questionable from a number of empirical perspectives.

REFERENCES

Aichhorn, A. (1925/1965) *Wayward Youth*. (Trans. E. Bryant, J. Deming, M. O'Neil Hawkins, G. Mohr, E. Mohr, H. Ross, and H. Thun). New York: The Viking Press.
Ansell, D. (2001). Where are we going tomorrow: Independent living practice. In K. A. Nolan and A. C. Downs (Eds.), *Preparing Youth for Long-Term Success*, 35-43. Washington, DC: Child Welfare League of America Press.

Barth, R. P. (1993). Promoting self-protection and self-control through life skill training. *Children and Youth Services Review*, 15, 281-293.

Bass, D. (1992). *Helping Vulnerable Youths: Runaway and Homeless Adolescents in the United States*. Washington, DC: NASW Press.

Beck, A. T., Freeman, A., & Associates. (1990). *Cognitive Therapy of Personality Disorders*. New York: Guilford Press.

Beelman, A., Pfingsten, U., & Losel, F. (1994). Effects of training social competence in children: A meta analysis of recent evaluation studies. *Journal of Clinical Child Psychology*, 23 (3), 260-271.

Calderra, P., & Merrell, K. W. (1997). Common dimensions of social skills of children and adolescents: A taxonomy of positive behaviors. *School Psychology Review*, 26, 265-279.

Cartledge, G., & Milburn, J. F. (1986). Selecting social skills. In G. Cartledge & J. F. Milburn (Eds.), *Teaching Social Skills to Children* (2nd ed.), pp. 7-28. New York: Pergamon Press.

Cartledge, G., & Milburn, J. F. (1995). *Teaching Social Skills to Children and Youth: Innovative Approaches* (3rd ed.). Needham Heights, MA: Allyn & Bacon.

Center on Children, Families, & the Law. (1994). *Independent Living Skills Evaluation: Former State Wards–Baseline Report*. Lincoln, NE: Author.

Cohler, B. J., & Zimmerman, D. P. (1997). Youth in residential care. From war nursery to therapeutic milieu. *The Psychoanalytic Study of the Child*, 52, 359-385. New Haven, CT: Yale University Press.

Cook, R. J. (1990). *A National evaluation of Title IV-E Foster Care Independent Living Programs for Youth: Phase 1*. (Contract No. OHDS 105-87-1608). U. S. Department of Health and Human Services. Rockville, MD: Westat, Inc.

Cook, R. J. (1994). Are we helping foster care youth prepare for their future? *Residential Treatment for Children & Youth*, 16 (3/4), 213-229.

Cook, R. J., & Ansell, D. I. (1986). *Independent Living Services for Youth in Substitute Care*. Rockville, MD: Westat, Inc.

Dowd, T., & Tierney, J. *Teaching Social Skills to Youth: A Curriculum for Child-Care Providers*. Boys Town, NE: The Boys Town Press.

Dygon, J. A. (1993). *The Culture and Lifestyle Appropriate Social Skills Curriculum: A Program for Socially Valid Social Skills Training*. New York: Wiley.

Elliott, S. N., & Gresham, F. M. (1991). *Social Skills Intervention Guide: Practical Strategies for Social Skills Training*. Circle Pines, MN: American Guidance Service.

Exner, J. E. (2000). *A Primer for Rorschach Interpretation*. Asheville, NC: Rorschach Workshops.

Freud, A. (1936/1966). *The Ego and the Mechanisms of Defense*. New York: International Universities Press.

Goldstein, A. P. (1988). *The Prepare Curriculum: Teaching Prosocial Competencies*. Champaign, IL: Research Press.

Goldstein, A. P., Glick, B., Reiner, S., Zimmerman, D., & Coultry, T. M. (1987). *Aggression Replacement Training: A Comprehensive Intervention for Aggressive Youth*. Champaign, IL: Research Press.

Goldstein, A. P., Sprafkin, R. P., Gershaw, N. J., & Klein, P. (1980). *Skillstreaming the Adolescent.* Champaign, IL: Research Press.

Grizenk, N., Zappitelli, M., Langevin, Jean-Philippe, Hrychko, S., El-Messidi, A., Kaminester, D., Pawliuk, N., & Stepanian, M. T. (2000). Effectiveness of a social skills training program using self/other perspective-taking: A nine-month follow-up. *American Journal of Orthopsychiatry, 70* (4), 501-509.

Hahn, A. The use of assessment procedures in foster care to evaluate readiness for independent living. *Children and Youth Services Review, 16* (5), 171-179.

Hartmann, H. (1939/1958). *Ego Psychology and the Problem of Adaptation.* (Trans. D. Rapaport). New York: International Universities Press.

Hoge, J., & Idalski, A. (2001). How Boysville of Michigan specifies and evaluates its supervised independent living program. In K. A. Nolan and A. C. Downs (Eds.), *Preparing Youth for Long-Term Success,* 83-93. Washington, DC: Child Welfare League of America Press.

Huggins, P. (1990-1995). *The Assist Program: Affective-Social Skills: Instructional Strategies and Techniques.* Longmont, CO: Sopris-West.

Lear, J. (1998). *Open Minded: Working Out the Logic of the Soul.* Cambridge, MA/London: Harvard University Press.

Lewin, K. (1943/1951). Defining the "field at a given time." In. D. Cartwright (Ed.) *Field Theory in Social Science,* 43-59. New York: Harper and Brothers.

Lewin, K. (1944/1951). Constructs in field theory. In. D. Cartwright (Ed.) *Field Theory in Social Science,* 30-41. New York: Harper and Brothers.

Lindsay, E. W., & Ahmed, F. U. (1999). The North Carolina Independent Living Program: A comparison of outcomes for participants and nonparticipants. *Children and Youth Services Review, 21* (5), 389-412.

Lochman, J. E., Curry, John F., Dane, H., & Ellis, M. (2001). The anger coping program: An empirically-supported treatment for aggressive children. *Residential Treatment for Children & Youth, 18* (3), 63-73.

McGinnis, E., & Goldstein, A. P. (1984). *Skillstreaming for the Elementary-Age Child.* Champaign, IL: Research Press.

McGinnis, E., & Goldstein, A. P. (1990). *Skillstreaming in Early Childhood: Teaching Prosocial Skills to the Preschool and Kindergarten Child.* Champaign, IL: Research Press.

Mech, E. V. (2001). Where are we going tomorrow: Independent living research. In K. A. Nolan and A. C. Downs (Eds.), *Preparing Youth for Long-Term Success,* 27-33. Washington, DC: Child Welfare League of America Press.

Mech, E. V., Ludy-Dobson, C., & Hulseman, F. S. (1994). Life-skills knowledge: A survey of foster adolescents in three placement settings. *Children and Youth Services Review, 16* (3/4), 181-200.

Merrell, K. W., & Gimpel, G. A. (1998). *Social Skills of Children and Adolescents: Conceptualization, Assessment, Treatment.* Mahwah, NJ/London: Lawrence Erlbaum Associates.

Milton, J. (2001). Psychoanalysis and cognitive behavior therapy–Rival paradigms or common ground? *International Journal of Psychoanalysis, 82* (3), 431-447.

Nollan, K. A., Wolf, M., Ansell, D., Burns, J., Barr, L., Copeland, W., & Paddock, G. Ready or not: Assessing youth's preparedness for independent living. *Child Welfare, 79* (2), 159-175.

Reddy, L. A., & Goldstein, A. P. (2001). Aggression Replacement Training: A multimodal intervention for aggressive adolescents. *Residential Treatment for Children & Youth, 18* (3), 47-62.

Redl, F., & Wineman, D. (1951). *Children Who Hate.* Glencoe, IL: The Free Press.

Redl, F., & Wineman, D. (1952). *Controls from Within.* Glencoe, IL: The Free Press.

Schneider, B. H. (1992). Didactive methods for enhancing children's peer relations: A quantitative review. *Clinical Psychology Review, 12,* 363-382.

Sheinker, J., & Sheinker, A. (1988). *Metacognitive Approach to Social Skills Training: A Program for Grades 4-12.* Frederick, MD: Aspen Publishers, Inc.

Shippensburg University Center for Juvenile Justice Training and Research. (1993). *An evaluation of Pennsylvania's Independent Living Program for Youth.* Shippensburg, PA: Author.

Stephens, T. M. (1978). *Social Skills in the Classroom.* Columbus, OH: Cedars Press.

Staddon, J. (2001). *The New Behaviorism: Mind, Mechanism, and Society.* Philadelphia, PA: Psychology Press.

Trapani, C. (1990). *Transition Goals for Adolescents with Learning Disabilities.* Boston/Toronto/London: Little-Brown.

U.S. General Accounting Office. (1994). *Residential Care: Some High-Risk Youth Benefit, But More Study Needed.* (Available from GAO, P.O. Box 6015, Gaithersburg, MD 20884-6015, USA).

White, R. B., & Gilliland, R. M. (1975). *Elements of Psychopathology: The Mechanisms of Defense.* New York: Grune & Stratton.

Whittaker, J. K. (2000). Reinventing residential childcare: An agenda for research and practice. *Residential Treatment for Children & Youth, 17* (3), 13-30.

Zimmerman, D. P., & Cohler, B. J. (1998). From disciplinary control to benign milieu in children's residential treatment. *Therapeutic Communities, 19* (2), 123-146. Reprinted in *Residential Treatment for Children & Youth, 18* (2), 27-54, 2000.

BIOGRAPHICAL NOTE

D. Patrick Zimmerman, PsyD, is Director of Admissions and Psychotherapy Services at the Sonia Shankman Orthogenic School and Lecturer, The Department of Psychiatry at the University of Chicago. He is also a member of the Senior Associate Faculty of the Illinois School of Professional Psychology/Chicago. Dr. Zimmerman is a graduate of the Chicago Center for Psychoanalysis and serves as a member of its Board of Directors.

A version of this paper was presented at the 45th Annual Meeting of the American Association of Children's Residential Centers, Atlanta, Georgia, October 19, 2001.

Correspondence may be sent to D. Patrick Zimmerman, The Orthogenic School, 1365 East Sixtieth Street, Chicago, IL 60637.

Index

Aggression Replacement Training (ART), 62,64
Aichhorn, August, xi-xii, 53,55,67
Anger Coping Program, 64
Ansell-Casey Life Skills Assessment, 57
Artificial intelligence studies, 66-67
Ashby, J., 50
Assessment inventories
  life-skills assessment, 57
  social-skills assessment, 60-61
ASSIST program (Affective-Social Skills: Instructional Strategies and Techniques), 63
Attention deficit hyperactivity disorder (ADHD), 16-17,64

Behavioral Assessment System for Children (BASC), 61
Behavioral disorders, 15-23
  classification, 16-17
  discussion, 20-21
  interventions, 17-18
  outcome variables, 18-20
Behavioral therapy, 67-68. *See also* Cognitive-behavioral therapy
Behaviorism, 67-68
Behavior rating scales, 60-61
Bellefaire/JCB. *See also* Transitional Living Program (Bellefaire/JCD)
  residential programs at, 38-39
  Transitional Living Program, 39-50
Bettelheim, Bruno, xiii-xv

Caretaker involvement, with sexually aggressive youth, 1-13. *See also* Treatment ally team
Case examples
  Familyworks program, 32-33
  sexually aggressive youth, 10
  Transitional Living Program (Bellefaire/ JCD), 40-45,47-48
(University of) Chicago Orthogenic School, xiv
CLASSIC (Culture and Lifestyle Appropriate Social Skills Intervention Curriculum), 62
Classical (Freudian) drive theory, 53
Cognitive-analytic therapy (CAT), 69
Cognitive-behavioral therapy, 66-69
  criticisms of, 66-67
  legacy of traditional, 67-68
  transitions in theory and technique, 68-69
Conduct disorder, 16
Copy theory of perception, 66-67

Daniel Memorial Independent Living Skills System, 57
Depression, 17
Developmental theories
  Erikson's, 71
  Kohlberg's theory of moral development, 71
  Piaget's, 70-71
  social-skills training and, 70-72
Deviancy training concept, 17
Didactic approach, in social-skills training, 70
Dowling, Scott, 50

Parent Management Training (PMT), 17
Parents. *See* Caregiver *entries;* Family
 entries
Perception, theories of, 66-67
Peterson, Mary, 23
Piaget's developmental theory, 70-71
Pioneer House, xiii, 55
Post-traumatic stress disorder (PTSD), 16
Prepare Curriculum, 62
Preschool Kindergarten Behavior
 Scales (PKBS), 61
Problem-solving skills training
 (PSST), 17
Psychiatry, historical aspects, xv-xvi

Redl, Fritz, xiii, xiv, 55
Relapse Presention Model (Gray &
 Pithers), 8-9
Residential treatment
 behavioral disorders, 15-23
 Familyworks program, 25-35
 historical perspective, xi-xvi, 52-55
 jurisdictional issues, xi-xii
 of sexually aggressive youth, 1-13
 social-skills and life-skills training,
  51-75
 Transitional Living Program
  (Bellefaire/JCD), 37-50
Risk factors, for sexually aggressive
 behavior, 4-5
River Oak Center for Children
 Familyworks Program, 25-35
Rorschach interpretation, Exner's
 system of, 71

Saunders, Suellen, 50
Scales of Independent Behavior, 57
Scales of Social Competence and School
 Adjustment (SSCSA), 61
Scanlan, Mark, 23
Sexually aggressive youth, 1-13
 focus of treatment, 2-4

treatment ally team, 4-5
treatment ally team group
 curriculum, 5-10
Skillstreaming series, 62
Social Skills Intervention Guide:
 Practical Strategies for
 Social Skills Training, 63
Social Skills Rating System (SSRS), 61
Social-skills training
 challenges, 69-77
 contemporary views, 59-63
 effectiveness, 63-67
 historical perspective, 52-55
 legacy of traditional therapies,
  67-68
 transitions in therapies, 68-69
State Individual Living Programs, 58

Teaching Social Skills to Youth: A
 Curriculum for Child-Care
 Professionals, 63
Tests of Everyday Living (TEL), 57
Transfer training, 65-66
Transitional Living Program
 (Bellefaire/JCD)
 case studies, 40-45,47-48
 discussion, 47-49
 evaluation methods, 45-46
 results, 46-47
Treatment ally team, 4-13
 case example, 10
 forming and establishing focus, 6-7
 planning, support, monitoring, 7-9
 programmatic guidelines, 10-12
 transition and testing, 9-10

Unconditional gratification, xv
University of Chicago Orthogenic
 School, xiv
University of Michigan Research
 Center for Group Dynamics,
 xiii